MW00947957

Should My Best-Friend be my Wife?

Written By : Derick Goldsby Jr.

TABLE OF CONTENTS

Author
Derick GoldsbyJr
Media tag :Shadow Soul
Dericksa18@Gmail.com
Instagram: Shadow Soull__
Youtube: Shadow Soul
Tiktok: Shadow Soul__

Chapter 1
Adolescents

I was taught at a young age to value love. I only accumulated three or four girlfriends within these quick 30 years of life. I don't love quickly. My mother told me if she didn't make me feel special and or didn't warm my heart to the point, I wanted to give her the world, leave her alone. I haven't genuinely given anyone but a fraction of my consciousness. Now a few might have received more significant portions than others, but in reality, they never had me.

My first was interesting. I didn't lose my Virginity till the junior year of high school; I watched all of my friend's brag about how much pussy they were getting not getting. While I, on the other hand, was boosting so I wouldn't look lame. But of course, anyone could see through my virgin face I was lying; hell, I looked twelve my entire high school career. And I was short, so I could see why I wasn't getting any play. Realizing my reality, I had to learn a better approach.' Let me think'; what was I good at naturally? I was good at talking to females when I treated them like best friends. So, if I treated Every potential like a best friend, I could put myself in a better position to get on in retrospect. From this point on, I made every girl I met my best friend so we could both be comfortable around each other. If I looked at you as a friend, it wasn't any pressure to have sex with you. I was shy and extremely nervous when I had to approach a girl, so when I told everyone, I had a girlfriend, it was like this unseen phenomenon. My friends were oozing with sarcasm, " finally, this man is about to lose his Virginity," " Derick said he's not leaving out of high school a virgin." The jokes never stopped, lol. I don't know how I ended up associating with these individuals, but these were the people I called my friends. The crew I still rock with to this day.

Fast forward a few months later; It was a half-day at school, and I decided to take advantage of the opportunity to sneak my girlfriend into the house to lose my Virginity. Perfect Plan; on the bus, I was calculating. My mom is currently at work, my sister still at school, house to myself for at least four hrs; I'm good! We got off the bus and walked three blocks to my house. I had a nosey neighbor, so before I approached my house, I had to make sure she wasn't home first. I told my girlfriend to wait a couple of houses down and wait for my signal. I walked around to the side door, then the front, close was clear. I waved for her to come. Of course, we didn't get right into it; we played fight, ate some food, and bullshitted as virgins do. Finally, I built up the courage to initiate contact. We were both nervous (side note, I didn't know how to put on a condom), but I knew what I was doing in my head. I watched an abundance of porn, but it never taught me how to put on a condom. I went to put it on, but something went wrong. I put it on backward, I think? But I was confused because I put it on the other way, and it still didn't fit. Now I'm looking like a true virgin. In my head, I think the condom was expired. I put the second one on, and it rips. At this point, I'm highly frustrated, and I'm having second thoughts of going in raw. My girl saw me struggling and suggested I grab the magnum. Puzzled and filled with a false sense of insecurity, My thoughts were, this girl wants me to embarrass myself by trying on this supergiant condom. But it was the last one; I had no choice. Reluctant, I put it on, and it was a perfect fit. I was astonished; I'm thinking to myself, " I got the gold stick," she's about to get this woody woodpecker TODAY." I felt a flawless type of confidence emerging after this discovery. This experience marked a day in history when no more short jokes could offend me. No one could make me feel a way about starting my sex life at 17. But, unfortunately, my excitement was short-lived. Losing your Virginity is a significant accomplishment in the male culture. But when I lost mine, it felt like another day. I haven't been this disappointed since I've learned wrestling was fake; I had a better time pleasing myself. But at the end of the day, I was no longer a virgin, and I was geeked about it. Suddenly the sound of keys entering the keyhole quickly wipes that grin right off my face.

I looked at the clock, it was only 2:30pm, and my mom was not supposed to be home for another two hrs. I was freaking out loudly; I heard my name being called from the living room. My girlfriend hopped up and asked me, " what are we gonna do?"I told her to find her panties, but she also had on a sundress, so she was okay. I, on the other hand, had to put on some draws and my basketball shorts quickly. As I was still deciding on a game plan, my mom's voice was getting louder and louder as she got closer to my door; my smart ass decided to wing it and meet her at my door. So I left the room and met my mom in the hallway; she quickly noticed something wasn't right. For one, my penis was still poking through my basketball shorts, and I couldn't even imagine my facial expression. She began to ask me what was wrong, and I said nothing as I tried to get her to change directions back down the hallway and into the kitchen. Her motherly instincts kicked in, and she hit me with a swim move like the joystick on madden. She opened my door, and my girlfriend was sitting on the bed watching tv, man my momma FLIPPED!!!! Her exact words were, " BITCH IF YOU DONT GET THE FUCK OUT OF

MY HOUSE BEFORE I FUCK YOU UP" I feared for her life; I have never seen my momma so red. She quickly left my room and told me to get the fuck out too "with my nasty ass"! You don't know the kind of fear I had in my soul; I Was praying that entire walk of shame on my way out the door. To make matters worse, my mom immediately gets on the phone and starts going off. She called both of my uncles to try to get them to talk some sense into me because I guess this was above her motherly guidance. And all they did was congratulate me and told me to be more careful. The cause and effect of wanting to stop getting hit with the virgin jokes at school? And see what the vagina feels like? fuck it; It was worth it!

I came back to school the next day a new man, but for most guys, after they lose their virginity, they go on a rampage. Not me, I called myself being in love. But I quickly learned this isn't love. It was just a new emotion that I wasn't used to. What I was feeling was lust; I felt that rush, that urge, that nerve to "make love" to a girl who didn't even love me. She has been cheating on me ever since the day I met her. She used me for my kindness, and this reality blinded me. Heartbroken and confused; I tried to move on from the situation the best way I could, which was to bang any girl in sight. I was young and full of emotions I didn't know how to manage. I let this temporary person rob me of my innocence.

"Innocence" (age 17)

"I never used to be this way; I was innocent. I didn't mind giving you my soul; I thought it was good to show a person you actually cared beyond control, but maybe because I was a virgin, I lack control; I didn't know the effects of sex yet. I didn't know our relationship would change because of this latex. I didn't know entering your walls would bring down all of my walls & Make me fall into this dangerous world of love, passion & pain; it's just sex? but I was innocent. Once we rolled over, I looked into your eyes & I knew you were the one; you had me, so submissive it was scary. If you said you were moving, I would have caught the next flight; you had me. Why can't this feeling last? How could you feel this strongly about a person & they don't feel the same in return? Walking around with their souls entwined with another, so you end up as another because their soul has been snatched by another, they need a replacement, ghostbuster, but I was innocent. The next day at school, I was eager to let the world know you were mine, my hs sweetheart you were, but you didn't want the title of being mine; I show up to your locker to kiss you & you put your hand over my mouth & say it's not the time, you declined. My innocence didn't prepare me for the emotional rollercoaster I was about to encounter. I was taken back from the lack of public affection, I didn't understand, but as soon as I even had a chance to confront you, your tongue was in the back of my throat, finally! Erasing my memory of all of your inconsistent behavior, you had me & nobody could tell me otherwise. It

*was the beginning of next week, and another opportunity sprung for us to have sex. it was a half-day & I was ready, still so inexperienced. Still, you couldn't tell me I wasn't that fresh hot & ready, ready to leave my mark. I laid you down on the couch in my basement then your phone rang. You told me it was your mother & you'll be right back. Moments later, you came back & told me you had to go, hashtag .... *silence *hurt .... Excuse me? Why? You told me you had to watch your little brother, who's not even out of school yet, & once again, my innocence plagued me. I just said, okay, this was some bs & then you proceeded to walk out the door with a smile on your face; at that moment, I grew a pair! I snatch her up before she stepped foot outside, I wasn't having it, I grabbed her phone & seen the truth, I went through her messages to see my baby calling another man baby saying "I'm on my way BABY" ...I threw her phone, slammed the door and shed tears of rage, I never use to be this way, why did she lie? So innocent to the fact that my mind ignored every Yield, lane changing, stop sign. I needed some air, but how could I replenish it? Who knew this was how today would finish & the scary thing about this is, it's a cycle that's never-ending; good guys turned to soulless souls & savages, nice girls turn into thots & men bashers, in this world, there's no hope for the innocent......"*

Getting inside another girl was my only solution. Luckily college was approaching, and I would be able to put my past struggles behind me and begin a new chapter in my life. College can allow me to become the man I was destined to be.

Chapter 2

The Introduction

Stepping foot on campus, I had no idea what to expect; the only thing I was sure of was that little Derick with no hoe's saga was over. I had to change that narrative, some people believe this was the moment I've changed, but in reality, I was evolving. My man's lance from high school was my roommate and was known for his savage ways, so I allowed him to teach me the savage lifestyle; I cared about female's feelings too much to the point that I'll let them walk all over me, friend-zone me, use my kindness for their benefit but never sexual. He would cuss me out whenever he saw me Being soft or falling back into my old ways. I needed it; I let girls cancel dates on me and still be the ones to text first. I was trapped in the thirst; I needed to pause and reverse.

Once we moved in, we noticed we had a plethora of females on our floor. So, we began scooping them out; later that day, we met some females at the cafeteria that happen to live in the same hall as us. It was this one girl that stood out from the rest, she just had a different aura about her & you couldn't help but notice her ass which you could see from the front, her name was Gemini. I knew I didn't have a chance, so I didn't say anything. My man's lance introduced us to the group of girls, and we sat down to eat with them. The rest is a blur, but somehow Gemini and I became the best of friends; it was scary how fast we clicked. It felt like we've been friends our entire lives. It was accelerated to the point we promised each other we wouldn't stay a part of each other's lives forever within the first months of the semester. Obviously, we've done this dance a few times in our past lives but that's a different story. Reason number one was because every guy on campus wanted her, and I didn't want to be a part of that population &

reason number two, she never had a guy best friend before, and that was my specialty. I figured

if I had a beautiful girl as a best friend, it could put me in situations to get on other appealing

women. From that moment on, you never saw us without each other, we spent nights together

sleeping in the same bed & nothing sexual ever occurred. I never wanted to ruin our friendship

because of a two second decision. We studied together, ate together, and went to events

together. Hell, she even used the bathroom with the door open. We were too comfortable with

each other.

Gemini ended up being my wingman; she was one of the bros. She made sure she put

me in an environment where situations could go down (as I predicted). I was surrounded by

women so often; people thought I was gay. But I was brilliant! I learned all the secret ways

around women; you don't learn about the opposite sex from the same sex, my bro's advice was

solid, but I learn the game from my female best friends. It made me more versatile; I had the

attitude of a gentleman but actions like a Fuck boy! Skills needed to survive in college. Usually,

when it was a lituation (a fun, exciting time), Gemini was involved in some way somehow.

As inseparable as we were, we never got intimate except for this one night. We just got

back to the dorms from a party & we were drunk as hell as we entered my room. I just wanted to

chill and watch some tv, but Gemini had other plans. She attacked me like a Lion & I was a

piece of meat; she crawled on me and reached for my main hood. I was so confused about what

was going on. I stop her in mid-motion. I knew she was drunk, so I gave her a pass, but I had to

clarify we're not about to do this tonight. She tried for several minutes till it began to register. For

a moment, it left her with a complex look on her face, 'no one had ever turned her down before,' she uttered & I was the first one. But as I begin to reflect, I believed she appreciated me more after that night because I was a gentleman & I saved our friendship, which was more important than sex to me. I loved her on a spiritual level that surpassed sex, I loved her with my soul & I didn't realize that at the time. The flip side to that was, I couldn't handle her sexually (Yet), and I was not about to embarrass myself. But it was evident that I cared about her. After that situation, it would be years later, after anything else occurred.

Even though I developed a stronger sense of confidence, I still had one major problem; I didn't know how to get out of the friend zone with girls I like. I learned how to be friends with women but haven't learned to harness that energy to use for my advantage; back in high school I had a friend named Stacy, she was an underclassman, but I liked her. We grew a close attachment to each other once I went off to college. We talk almost every night on the phone. She trusted me so much she gave up her virginity to me. I never took someone's Virginity, so I didn't know what to expect. All I knew was that when you take a girl's Virginity, they fall madly in love with you, and they chase after you like a lost puppy.

Well, at least that's what was seen on TV. But obviously, I was mistaken because the complete opposite transpired. After it happened, I could have sworn to you I was in love (again). I would have done any and everything for this girl, coming home on the weekends to be with her, walks to the gas station carrying her on my back because her feet hurt. I enjoyed making her happy, but she didn't feel the same, it was like the roles were reversed. She was notably nonchalant with her actions; it hurt me because I took a girl's Virginity, and I still couldn't escape the friend zone. What was wrong with me? At the time, I didn't consider her age and how she didn't understand the level of love I offered her. She even went around the HS telling other people someone else took her Virginity. Stuck in my feelings, I had to swallow yet another "L" (Lost). The late-night phone conversation wasn't as flavorful & I was losing interest. How do you get friend zone by a first-year student while taking Her Virginity? Then ask for consoling for the guy she friend-zoned me for? Ooooh, the pain; I can't believe you gave an underclassman our special moment.

"Special moment" (age 18)

" I want you to take my virginity," you told me; I was shocked but happy, finally, our special moment. The way you felt for me was how I felt for you; tell me what the missing component was? Once we shared our moment, it was beautiful, eyes watering, but I wiped the tears before they fell to keep mine from forming. Once we shared souls, I was in love; I was on cloud 9. Above anything that I did not love, the thought of you not feeling the same never pop up. But if that was the case, we were supposed to be hand & hand, but now I'm on the chase, chase to claim what's mine, but I got replaced. Replaced by the guy you were talking to, you gave him our special moment, wait? Are you serious? Are you going to let this lie follow suit? I was in love with you. I'm the one that took your Virginity, but to the world, it was him now I'm number 2. Masked in this role I was forced to play, talking to you, smiling at you like everything is okay, knowing damn well I'm lying, but the risk of me mentioning my feelings & getting rejected again? I was like, no way. I swallowed my pride & said, okay, I know the truth; we had our moment. I don't need any proof, he can shout it to the mountain tops, but you know the truth. But I'm brave enough to take it; it's like you took my soul & kept it then gave yours to him. I pray he accept it cause karmas a bitch, but I'll try to protect it, protect it from coming after you by giving my okay to let you do you. You might not love me the same as much I do, but I'll always stay true & I'll never forget our special moment I gave to you."

Added, I eventually got over it, but it sucked in the beginning; by the way she was telling the truth about someone else taking her virginity. I just charged it to the game. Stacy was younger, and I had to realize it's not the right time and to remain friends. Luckily, I was away at college, so I had a variety of others to distract me. During the rest of my semesters, I gradually build up my bone collection. Don't judge me on the women I was selecting; my self-esteem/ confidence wasn't as high as it is now, so I accumulated a few linebacker/ Kermit the frog looking chicks to my roster. We all gotta start somewhere. I had to get my reps up, and less appealing girls were easier to concur.

Remember when I called Gemini my wingman? In retrospect, I was hers as well; see, she didn't have a phone at the time, so the guys that tried to get in contact with her had to go through me. We shared my phone; she had it more than me. When my conquest called, she'll answer, and no one ever had a problem with her, it was crazy. Her personality was very inviting. When her males messaged her, they knew it was my phone. They would ask permission to talk to her (on my phone), I reiterate. Then the question always arose, " don't you date that little nigga you be with all the time'? It seemed like Gemini had to answer that question every other week. And of course, all of my friends and everyone that knew me either thinks I'm hitting it or gay for not. But I didn't care what others thought. We had each other back. Even though we have only known each other for a school year, I'll do anything for her. I truly felt I made a lifelong friend that will be in my inner circle for eternity.

Chapter 3
Crazy love

As we were leaving school for the summer, I started to reflect on my year. I had an amazing, crazy school year. Between the threesomes & many one-night stands, I felt like a changed man. Being on my own for the first time was life-changing. Trying to balance a social life with your studies was half the battle. Picture trying to study for an exam you have to take in the morning, and half-naked girls barge into your room, forcing you to drink. I think the most embarrassing situation that occurred was when I threw up before sex. I did that a few times actually; I was a lightweight trying to hang with the big boys. I was also that guy that got drunk as hell and kissed random girls I just met. I used to get so drunk my roommate frequently put me on his shoulders like an infant to carry me home. I'll never forget that true friendship. I remember when the crew and I went college hopping to several universities, so many memories. The one that stuck out the most was when we had got into a brawl at that one college. It was chaos, but my squad and I held our own. You can't call yourself friends if you have never been through situations that test loyalty. Making sure we all left the party with little to no scratches was a blessing. I don't need an entourage; I need a few wolves who won't back down. If I didn't learn anything my first semester, I learn loyalty. It was bittersweet because I was leaving my best friend. Also, we both didn't have cars, so we weren't going to see each other for the entire summer. She also didn't have a phone, but she manages to reach out to me frequently throughout the summer with social media and random phone numbers. This is how it was for us for a while, for the long-distance, I mean. Due to financial reasons, I couldn't make it back to school for the following school year & my bf lost touch temporarily. It devastated me because I felt like a failure. My grades were good enough to advance, and my mother just wasn't poor enough to get the extra financial funds I needed to stay. I didn't want my friendship to die, but I guess this would be our first test to see how resilient our friendship was.

During this time, I recently reconnected with an old high school friend. We used to text frequently while I was away at school, and she was excited that I was back in the city. Her name was Lay, and she was a senior when I was a junior. We flirted immensely, and she was always a calm ass person to kick it with. During the summer, we started talking and decided to start as friends (per usual) because she had a boyfriend. We spent the majority of the summer catching up and sharing college experiences and embarrassing stuff we did.

The new school year has begun & since I wasn't going back to my university, I had to apply for community college. Meanwhile, Lay was at her university getting back settled. It's crazy for a split second; she replaced Gemini as my best friend. We talked every day, all day like she didn't have a boyfriend. I knew what I was doing; I wanted to be the guy your girl told you not to worry about. And before you know it, one day she called me crying, telling me how her boyfriend was cheating on her and she wanted to kill him. I encouraged her to try to leave, but she chose to stay. In reality, she plotted revenge (this would be frequent in this chapter. Just wait on it). Lay had come home for a weekend & we went to this house party her friends were throwing from high school.

It was lit; everyone was just vibing, having a good time. I immediately started throwing back shots as If my liquor tolerance skyrocketed overnight. Somehow Lay and I ended up alone in the downstairs laundry room. And since I had liquor courage, I picked now to make my move. The sounds of kissing, moans, and music painted a scene of intimacy; while everyone was upstairs partying, I was busy trying to penetrate. I lifted her on top of the washing machine and processed to take her clothes off. She abruptly stopped me because she heard voices. I was being cock block by some of the guys at the party trying to record us. Man, I was so mad, but once they got hip to the fact, we knew they were there, they scattered. I convinced her to start again, this time, we were on the floor, and coincidently her phone had her boyfriend on the line right next to us. She called him while we were in the middle of trying to have sex, and he heard it. The kissing, the moaning, the shit-talking, it was getting heated. Then her friends came downstairs to cock block me some more. Nobody wanted me to be great. They came downstairs trying to persuade her to smoke, which she accepted and told me she would be right back. she played with me, I waited so long I ended up going to sleep. I was convinced she used me for revenge. So, I got up, went back upstairs to the party, where I passed out drunk, & threw up all over the floor. It wasn't good. Even If I was going to get some pussy, I shut the door on that for the night. My friends ended up carrying me out of the party, into the car, and the house. My mom's told them they should have left me in the door like the dude from "house party".

Months later, lay and I continued to talk, and on top of that, she decided not to go back to school for the winter semester, so we got even closer. Eventually, we would end up in a relationship. Lay was a good girl, but I ignored all her sneaky, vindictive, and evil ways because I was just convinced, she wouldn't do that to me. I had every intention of treating her right. We were together for a year and six months, I believe, and it was a life-changing experience, that's for sure. We started like any other normal relationship. Late-night phone calls, constant communication like it's the last day yawl will ever speak. I didn't have a car, so we had to car pull & use our parents to get around, but we made it happen. Afterwhile, it got repetitive, and Lay was growing tired of not having a car. I believe her exact words were, " I'm tired of this high school-ass relationship" She was right. I had to find the courage and get a car. So, for about three months, I had to grind at my minimum wage job to stack for a car. She helped motivate me to get my first car; it was a 2001 Malibu, but it was clean, I tell you. So, since we had a car now the problems, we thought we had failed to the waste side. Everything seems like it was going perfectly; she cashed out on me for Christmas. We went out every weekend; I was happy. This one day, out of the blue, she told me she was going away to some physiatrist's hospital for therapy for the weekend. I was puzzled, I knew she had a history of seeing a therapist based on what she told me, but I didn't believe it. She convinced me that she was serious and wouldn't be able to talk to me because she wasn't allowed to have her phone, crazy right? But I played along, not believing shit she said. So, the weekend arrives, and she takes off.

Everything was going according to plan for her till randomly, her ex followed me on Twitter. I notice he was sub-tweeting, talking shit, saying how his ex-chick is in his room, and "her nigga weak," just a bunch of trash to get me riled up. Filled with embarrassment and anger, I lashed out! I blew her phone up with text/ calls; you name it. Then I tried to get her ex to show me proof that she was there, he never did. So, I was confused; her story didn't add up for shit, and then magically, her ex was saying she was at his school. That made more logical sense to me, so I was convinced she was cheating on me. I should have ended the relationship right there just off my gut feeling, but I didn't. I Didn't have enough proof, but I lost all trust in Lay that day. I mentally began to wander off.

I kept in contact with Stacy after the whole virginity thing; we stayed friends and frequently talked, sometimes even sexually. She was the girl you lie to and tell your girl you guys have nothing going on, and the friendship is strictly platonic. All lies, she had a hold on me I couldn't shake, we had a soul tie, and I never felt bad for me cheating on Lay with her. I slept with Stacy twice during my relationship with Lay. I convinced Stacy that Lay and I were on a break so she wouldn't feel guilty of being a homewrecker. If Stacy had told me she was in love with me, I would drop that next second. That's how strong my feelings still were. But I knew that never would happen; it was a beautiful fantasy with no real chance of coming true. So, I decided to stop, I was only going to continue to get my feelings hurt, and on top of that, I felt like I achieved my goal of getting some internal revenge on Lay. In a sinister way, I felt cleanse enough to refocus on my relationship again.

As soon as I started rebuilding the trust that was lacking in our relationship, another girl entered the picture. Her name was jasmine. Jasmine was a girl I met at Saginaw when my boys and I use to college hop. I met her through mutual friends. I can't lie. She was fine as hell; I told myself if I ever got a shot, I would take it. She ended up throwing a house party; she, too, had a boyfriend at the time. So, my friend Kells and I went, and it was fun, minus her damn dog eating at my feet the whole time. We exchanged Skype names, funny right? After that party, we would Skype all the time. When I wasn't with my girlfriend, I would Skype jasmine playing the whole best friend role. I don't know how I had all this free time to talk to other women, but I did & I took advantage. I was slowly not giving AF about my relationship; I was just in it for the benefits. Once I lose my trust in you, the relationship is beyond repair. But since Lay was like a bf to me, that kept us together for as long as we did. Our first anniversary was coming up & I was excited to plan it. I had a romantic dinner set up & I also had a room with a jacuzzi hot tub. Everything was going as planned, then suddenly the unexpected happened. All the side flirting and talking to jasmine granted me the opportunity to have sex with her. I knew I wasn't going to pass that up. She was the finest girl that wanted to have sex with me, and I didn't think twice about doing it. My anniversary date was a day away, and I was about to risk it all. Jasmine came over the morning before, and I would tell you it was great, but it wasn't. I wasn't mentally ready, my condom kept drying up, and my penis stayed flaccid. I felt like a virgin all over again. It was like she made me lose my confidence. Hands down, I put on my worst performance. I embarrassed myself so badly I felt it was immediate karma. Afterward, I apologize; I knew it was terrible, but maybe I could redeem myself? She quickly declined and told me that would never happen again and left my house. Lucky that wouldn't be our final encounter. And to make matters worse, she left a vast Hickey on my neck, and I have an anniversary date tomorrow!!! This mark was so massive my mother and sister had to put make-up on my neck. I love them forever for that, actual ride or die.

The next day arrives, and its date night; it was successful. The plan was to get her so drunk in the jacuzzi if the make-up wore off, she wouldn't remember, and she didn't, and I was danger-free. But after that night, my conscience started to speak to me, I was becoming fatigued, and this cheating was begging to wear on me. A month later, I developed the maturity to tell Lay I cheated on her three times with two different girls. I suspected that she suspected that I was doing something, but just like our previous situation, she didn't have any proof. But the difference between her and I was she came out and asked me was I hiding anything. She convinces me that she wouldn't be mad. She just wants to know the truth. A clear trap that I failed for. She was heartbroken, and she broke up with me. I deserve it; even If I had my suspicions of her, it didn't make it right for me to go out and cheat. I was also 20-21 years old; I should be spending my 20's exploring and trying to figure out what I like so I can prevent shit like this from happening. But I learned from this experience, and foolishly she ended up taking me back under one condition. She wanted to try an open relationship, and the rules were since she was bi-sexual, she could sleep with girls, and I can sleep with whoever I want as long as I discuss it with her first and always use a condom. At the time, I thought the arrangement was perfect. But shortly, I began to hate it.

One night I went through her phone. I saw her getting nudes from a girl, and it made me so hot my mindset was as if I saw a dick pic. I snapped at her and told her I couldn't handle an open relationship, and I just wanted her. I promise I'll never cheat on her again. (Translation)I didn't want to see her with anyone else. And she agreed to squash the agreement. Getting back to normal, during that spring, we decided to get an apartment together—my first apartment. The struggles of having sex at her grandma's house were over. We could finally be together alone!! Yearning for this freedom since college, I was going to capitalize. Moving in with the opposite was also a life-changing choice I made that taught me a great deal of humility.

Most of our parents believe that you shouldn't move in with someone unless you are married; I always felt that was stupid and illogical. I understand religious reasoning, but living with someone is entirely different from spending the night with each other. You get to introduce yourself to a different person. Just like no sex before marriage, how do you know this is someone you want to spend the rest of your life with if you never experience these massive deal breakers? I'll be damned if I married someone without checking boxes. When we moved in, I found out that she hates cleaning and washing dishes, and she only did it because I was coming over. The dark and unattractive secrets come out when you sign that lease. I loved that my family was concerned, but I had to experience this milestone my way. So, when we first moved, I was led to believe that we were going to have sex all the time and be overly joyed in our own little space. But tragically, it goes straight south from here. Her excuse for not wanting to have sex with me was because her depo shot was affecting her sex drive (which I found out later that depo shot was the devil), and she lacks the motivation to want to do anything. Now you imagine being 21 with your apartment with your girlfriend and getting little to no sexual stimulation? What did you think was going to happen? Now the mature me would have got her off the depo shot and just weathered the storm, but needless to say, I was 21. I swore faithfulness because I felt like I had a moral obligation to stay true to my word, but I needed some excitement, which isn't shit of me because I ponder what if something was wrong with her body? My mindset was as she was playing me and most likely having sexual relations with someone else. As much as I wanted to trust her, my male intuition was screaming at me. Once again, I had another opportunity to end the relationship, but I suggested we try the open relationship again. We just moved into the apartment. The pride in me couldn't let my mother know she was right (about moving in with her). I secretly had this girl named raven I was trying to reconnect with. I guess you can say she was a childhood crush; we moved away from each other right before it was time for middle school, and I haven't seen her ever since. Still being neglected, lay unconsciously or consciously open the door for raven to come in. technically, with our new rules, I wasn't in the wrong in having a side chick, but I didn't trust that lay genuinely agreed with the agreement. I decided to keep raven my little secret. Females can tell when you're giving your attention to someone else. My apartment never felt like a home; it was surrounded by tension, awkward silence, and distrust. I felt like I was single with a roommate. The final icing on the cake was when raven reluctantly decided to inform me that she had chlamydia and that I should get checked out. She earns some respect by approaching me in person and telling me to my face. I couldn't imagine how hard that had to be, but I honestly didn't give a fuck. I damn near caught a case and put her through her damn window when she told me. I had to relax and just take the L; it was part my fault. I should have had a condom on. I thought I never would experience an std; I felt dirty and betrayed. How dare my side chick unveil unfaithfulness in my time of need. But she also owed no loyalty to me, and I played with her emotions like a game of dominoes. So, my karma had its way with me, and I deserved every lesson. My only concern was making sure Lay didn't find out. But that dream was short-lived; Henry Ford ended up sending my test results to the house when I wasn't home. Lay called me while I was at work and said, " so you have a letter here from Henry ford" I played it off like it wasn't anything and told her, "Just leave it on the table. I'll look at it when I get home." Then she proceeded to tell me she opened it. " Nigga you got chlamydia??" And you got a tract infection?" I was unprepared and caught off guard, so my response was 'who the fuck is chlamydia? I never met her before", she busted me, and I didn't know how to handle it. I was afraid to go home; I was in foreign territory. Surprisingly She was acting normal, at least for a week. But I knew it was just a matter of time before she exploded. It was just the calm before the storm. For that entire week, I slept with one eye closed.

      I came in the house high on a Friday night and lay questioning my whereabouts; I did not feel like talking. I just wanted to go to sleep, but she wasn't allowing it. She began to raise her voice while I continued to walk away from her. She then came into the room and slapped this black plastic lap that was by the bed into my face. Glass shattered, but it didn't cut my face. I blackout; I chimed her up by her shirt against the wall, then I quickly snapped out of it. I had to get out of there. But not before she got some revenge for all my cheating and bullshit. She unleashed every ounce of her harnessed negative energy and just snapped on me. This was the first time I was involved in domestic violence. Remind you I'm high as fuck, so usually, I would have been able to guard my face and hold her down. Her adrenaline was at her max today because She was connecting like Tyson. I was just trying to grab some of my belongings before I left, but she hit me every step of the way. I manage to get her out of the room and lock it while I grab my stuff. Then it gets even wilder; she kneeled on the floor with a towel and a lighter. She was going to set me on fire, and we were on the third floor. It was too high up to jump out the windows without hurting myself. My only option was to prevent her from burning the apartment down; I opened the door, picked her up, and slammed her so I could free the lighter out of her hands. she swore I just beat her ass. She became hysterical; I believe I was in a potential snapped situation. I called my mom to let her know I'm on my way. She heard lay in the background being emotionally loud. So, she told me to hurry home don't catch a case in Farmington (outskirts city from Detroit). Doing 90mph to my mom's crib, I was a little emotional; I can't believe I just went through all of that. I had no one to blame but the person in the mirror.

I finally made it home; my momma and sister were heated; they were ready to ride out. But I called off the dogs. I made my bed and now I have to LAY in it. After things cooled down, I went back to the apartment to grab the rest of my things, filled with guilt. Even after she put her hands on me, I felt I deserved it. She didn't hurt me, so it was easy to shrug off. In all reality, I didn't want to move back with my mother. Half of that apartment was mine, all the bills were in my name, so I was just trying to figure out a way to be cordial. I asked for her forgiveness, and eventually, she granted my wish, but it was a hidden clause. Just like her last relationship, she wanted revenge on me. She decided to mess with someone we both knew from our high school. She wanted to rub it in my face to make me jealous. At that moment, I realized this was an unhealthy relationship. It wasn't worth it; I rather just stay home with my moms and regather myself. I lasted not even six months in that apartment, but I don't regret anything. As I reflect, I'm glad we weren't having sex because what If I got her pregnant? I needed that experience; it taught me about karma & never love because of convincing.

"LPI" (age 20- 21)

"Loyalty, priority, initiative, do you ever question your relationship? Or wonder what is missing? What did you build your relationship on? Was it sex? best friends that ended up catching feelings? The Internet? You know the usual... It's getting harder to distinguish what's real & what's temporary these days. The grass is getting higher & these snakes are getting harder to see, but don't be afraid; if you follow LPI, you'll be okay.

LOYALTY- Do your significant other put the world on notice that you are committed? Do he put his old flings In check if they disrespect? Do you have to question what they are doing when yall not together? How tight is your bond if all he has to do is like a girl picture & you tripping? Or if she goes out with her friends & you questioning her the whole time she's out? Well, if you're loyal, you won't have trust issues; never give him/her a seed to plant because once you lost the loyalty & trust, how can the relationship ever thrust?

Priority- does he always go out with his boys & leave you at home? Does she always have time for everyone else's problems & busy giving relationship advice & can't even fix her own? It's easy to feel not wanted or insecure in a relationship if you don't tend to your partner, your priorities must be in order & keep In-mind you all in this together, just be respectful and courteous.

Initiative- does he take the initiative & take you out just because or just because of gifts? Does she take care of business without you even asking, do you do for each other because it's second nature? Do you plan things out? Or is everything just flows with the wind? I can tell you right now if I have to ask for anything sexual, you're not the one; you have to be able to take the initiative; it means more to your significant other. They will feel unique & more critical, just like how they should feel.

LPI should be the building block on any relationship; it's all about building a solid foundation that won't break because of a flawed argument or social media misunderstandings. If a home concrete foundation isn't strong, how can it withstand a dangerous storm? Only the strong will survive, so why not do everything in your power to make sure your relationship also survives any storm that it will face?"

Chapter 4
Why is opportunity blind?

Due to this latest event, I knew I wouldn't be in another serious relationship for a while. And you probably notice that I didn't mention Gemini at all in that last chapter. During the relationship with Lay, we barely communicated. Gemini and I friendship weren't relationship friendly, and I don't mean it as if she tries to disrespect my relationship by any means or vice versa. We were so tight I felt it would make our partners uncomfortable due to us being the opposite sex. When we're both in relationships, we tried to distance ourselves. And it was crazy because when we did talk, it would be a 5-hour conversation, then it would be weeks or months before I heard from her again. But I loved every second. My last relationship taught me I wasn't ready for commitment. I wasn't ready to live with the opposite sex, and I'm still in my twenties. I barely had a hoe phase; I needed to get out there and live my best life. In all honesty, I feel everyone should have a phase in their life where they experience multiple "situations (Responsibly)". It will help you learn what you like and don't like in a future partner.

I never was known as the "approach" type when it came to getting girls. I was the laid-back and chill type of guy, a big flirt. I let my sinister smile and funny, gentlemen-like personality guide me. As I flashback, I remember this one girl at my old job I had a massive crush on. She was strapped (slim thick - thick, female), thick in all the right places, tiny waist. She worked next door, so I flirted with her every chance I got. I convinced her to work with me, and she agreed after some months of failed attempts. After I got her hired in, I flossed a little since I was one of the managers I had pulled. Eventually, that led to me getting a date. I decided I wanted to do something out of my norm. I took her to the black rock in Novi and go-cart racing after that. Of course, I paid for it all, and I didn't expect any ass after. Well, I mean, I was hoping, but it still didn't lead my mind to believe so. After the date I took her home, we had a cool pleasant talk on the way to her house. I believe I asked her how the date was? She replied, "the date was really nice. Nobody has ever taken me out on a real date like that in a while, but maybe we should just stay friends!" I'm like, ooooooooooooouch! My heart, this damn friend zone shit, I can't take it. How do I get looked at as a savage??? Was it my height? My babyface? What was it?? I called Gemini and told her what happened. She just simply told me I was too nice. That shit still confuses me to this day? Am I too nice?

<u>"Friendzone" (age 21)</u>

"Is it my fault that I can't help but act like I like the person I actually like? I don't know how to mask the emotions I get when I'm around you. I want to buy you the world. If I could have it to where your feet never have to touch the ground, I would make it happen. You have my undivided attention, but it's only one problem. You don't want it. I'm too trustworthy. I'm too nice. I'm too much of a FRIEND. I'm the guy you describe every day to me that you need in your life. & I have to get into character & play this friend zone role because you can't open up your eyes & realize I'm the reflection you see in the water, but you rather skip rocks in it. How do I escape this cage you lock me in without losing our friendship. I love you, but you just call me your bro? That shit hurt; it feels like my heart is made out of glass & you smashed it & made me pick up the broken pieces with my bare hands

cutting me even more profound. & Maybe you might feel the same, but I will never know because every time I gather up my confidence to ask you, finally, you asked me for advice on another man. I can't help that I'm easy to talk to & get advice from. I'm just being the man you want but will never see me as your man, just a friend that you can always fall back on when you're about to fall. Still, it's ironic that you're the one knocking me down & you'll never catch my fall, & maybe one day you will, but then again, why should I keep getting my hopes cloud high for you to squeeze the rain out of it... Let me just stay in my own zone, the safe zone, the zone that works out for everybody .... The FRIEND ZONE"

I'm just not a mean guy, but I had to be to get the respect I wanted. After college, I made the conscious decision to be an asshole, just don't give a fuck (AF) about shit. Somehow, I've lost sight of that, but it's time to reactivate. Don't text her back, don't care about her feelings, don't share your feelings, just stick and move. I can't believe that method worked. Reflecting now, I apologize to girls I've hurt in that process but something had to shake. A few of the good girls didn't deserve this treatment, but it's always some casualties in war. Modern-day relationships were for the birds, and I'm as cold as winter.

"Modern-day relationship (age 21)

"I met a girl. We converse, we laugh, we had a good time. She gives me her number & tells me not to be a stranger & to hit her up sometimes. I say ok, we hug & part ways. Later the next day, I sent her a text, "hey Tiffany, it's Derick from last night" she texts back with all smiles & replies, "I've been waiting on your text; what's up?" I say last night was fun. We should do it again sometime & she agrees. So, a week later, we go out, get some drinks & relax in a calm, laid-back environment. We're talking for a while, eating then she asked me a question." what are your intentions with me?" I reply, "nothing, I just wanna enjoy another adult's company & have some adult fun, nothing serious" is that cool with you? She replies, yes, that's great. I can do that!.

PAUSE, STOP EVERYTHING!!!!!

Why can't it stay like this? When a guy hits you with those lines, believe him he doesn't want a relationship and if you're genuinely not with it, be honest with yourself and get yourself out of the situation. Why do females have to advance & ask what we are? What is this leading to? Why can't you just let it ride? Oh, because you want a relationship now, feelings change. I have to be in a relationship with you because of how you feel? I'm sorry I'm everything you want in a guy, I'm sorry I'm a gentleman, I'm sorry I have Toxic sex; having a girlfriend is the farthest thought from my mind. If I'm consistent, why question what we do? Now you're forcing my hand to either cut you off

or having you do the same to me because I don't want to adapt &
make you the one-in only person in my life? Now I get scrutinized
because "she's a good girl, why not make her yours?" Because I don't
want tooooooo , is it a crime to want to stay single & meet people? If
something evolves between us, then let it happen. If you feel like I'm
stringing you along & you're wasting your time, then leave. You always
have that option, but I don't think you should blame me for not feeling
the same way you're feeling! Yes, I want to have relations. Yes, I want
to hang out, laugh & have a great time, but does that mean I have to
commit to you? Why?? "you're too old to have hoes" I don't have
hoes; I have several women that sparks my interest & I feel like I don't
have to settle for any particular one & I'm only 21, maybe 5-6years
from now I might want to become a family man. Still, I'm not there yet
& don't bash me & try to make me feel less of a man because of my
reality! If you can't take it? Bounce! At least you can't say I didn't keep
it honest & I wasn't upfront with you. "

Best friend, on the other hand, was like me when it came to relationships. She didn't
have a lot of relationships, but when she did, it was serious. She used to tell me every particular
detail she did for her boyfriends. None of them actually deserve it, but that was the kind of
person she was. A real people pleaser but never received the same kind of appreciation in
return. It was always one-sided. For example, she can take you on a helicopter ride and take
you on a wine venue tour. Things that actually require some thought. And what does she
receive in return? A piece of jewelry, if that, no effort nor thought.

32

On top of that, she gets cheated on, misunderstood, and ends up taking care of every grown man she's been with. She's so used to being in charge of the relationship I thought it would be hard for her to fall back and let a man be a man. But I found out later in life what the real deal was.

When my best friend graduated from college, we picked back up where we last left off. Things are different now. I had a car, some facial hair may be an inch taller, maybe not, and she was gorgeous! I haven't seen her in almost four years, but I looked at her through a different lens the Day I drove up to visit. She took me to a hotel she managed. It was beautiful to see her in this working, boss-like atmosphere. It gave me an uncomfortable feeling because this was the first time in my life, I saw us being together. But I didn't want to spring that on her. I didn't want to make things awkward, fear of rejection, and also, she had a boyfriend. But internally, I couldn't deny the emotions. April 15th, 2015, was the transitional state for me emotionally.

After the tour of the hotel, we just hung out. We went to the mall. I decided I wanted to start dressing more casually. She assisted me by buying me my first set of blazers and some fresh button-ups! She was my future stylist. After that, I facetime her every time I jump fresh to make sure I was good to go. Later that night, we slept in the same bed together, no different than college. We slept together millions of times, sometimes just in our undergarments. But today was strange. Today I felt myself erecting in the middle of the night. After hours of tossing and turning nervously, I wonder how she felt. I brushed my penis up on her to get a reaction, silence, no reaction. In my head, it's not a rejection. Maybe she was just sleeping extremely hard, so I tried it again. She then turned around and asked me what I was doing and to get my

33

dick off of her. I quickly apologized and hit her with the, "I'm sorry I was asleep." Shot my shot and didn't even graze the rim. This was one of many future awkward moments we would share together. Of course, morning comes, and we both awaken as if nothing happened. Still awkwardness in the air, I chose to break it by asking her to breakfast before leaving to go back to the city. She agreed, and we enjoyed our breakfast like good friends laughing and vibing like normal. After breakfast, I hit the road back to Detroit. The whole ride, I'm thinking, "She just got out of a relationship with someone she loved. It was dumb of me to express my feelings now", even though I didn't express any verbally, my actions hinted that I wanted more than friendship. But knowing my best friend, she just brushed it off because she didn't want to ruin our friendship. After that visit and just reminiscing on our 5–6-year relationship. I was convinced I had real feelings for her, but I have to Harbor them till the right time.

Chapter 5
Growth is a slow process

Remember when I told you hadn't seen the last of jasmine? After the horrible sex experience, we nurtured a platonic friendship. No, let's be honest, she friend zones the hell out of me. So deep, she said I'm more like her brother. "Not the brother line," and for a while, I would've done anything for a second shot, but being friends was cool. We became so adhesive she gave me a key to her apartment. I used to crash there before and after work. It was even nights that we slept together. Because of Gemini, I was able to do that. Spending so much time with a person, I started to fall for her. I didn't want to, especially when I found out she hit one of my friends. I had to find out through other people, and showed me what kind of person she was. Of course, she didn't owe me anything. We were friends. She can do what she wants. I'll never fight over a female especially if she doesn't belong to me in the first place, so I buried that. I kept it as a reminder to never get too close and to not forget the disrespect.

The following spring, we decided to plan a trip for her birthday out of the country. She had all of these people raising their hands to go, but of course, you know how black people are when planning a trip. One by one, as the time got near for us to go, people started to flake. Till no one was left but me and jasmine. I still wanted to go. I had never been out of the country. Jasmine thought I would flake too, so she was about to cancel it, but I prevented her. I told her I'll cover the extra cost so we can still go, and we did. It looked like a baecation to everyone else, but we were just living our best life as friends. I even slept with someone else on the trip. Skinny dipping, ruining other people's relationships, fuck it. We did what we wanted to do with no regrets. We had the time of our lives, and after we made it back to the city, everything seemed to change. Now we're like super best friends. Everything was excellent until her friend Jessica pop into the picture. She was fine as hell, and she thought I was cute. I took this opportunity to get back at jasmine for smashing one of my boys. Well, that was my initial thought. Then it transitions to "she was fine" I want to fuck regardless. So, when I told Jasmine I was about to, she looked devastated. Why would I do something like that? Like She had the right to feel anyway? But I knew what I was doing, I was just planting my seeds. A few weeks later, Jessica and I got a room and hooked up, and it was great. So great that we set up another session. I Thurley enjoyed myself, Jasmine didn't like that one bit, but she'll never tell me. She chalked it up as revenge and moved on, well, not quite. She felt away about Jessica afterward. I don't believe Jessica was a lousy friend. I'm pretty sure Jasmine told her that we were just friends, and she didn't have any feelings for me. Now, if Jasmine was lying, then that's her fault, but I wasn't satisfied for some strange reason. Obviously, I'm in my feelings, and I didn't realize it at the time.

Jasmine had another friend named Bubble that I occasionally talk to to help with relationship advice and whatnot. Jasmine introduces us via call. This one particular day, Bubbles had contacted me to ask me if I could help her friend out with a situation. She needed some advice about a guy, and I was the man for the job. But what Jasmine didn't know, we continued to talk heavy after that. The connection was getting thick. She was cool but was also an opportunist. One Day, we talked on the phone about situationships, and Jasmine and my bro name were brought up. I guess this was the moment I revealed to someone that I cared and her actions hurt me. Also, around that time, bubbles and Jasmine weren't talking. So, she proceeded to tell me why their relationship changed for the worse and why she wanted to get revenge. The situation was a bunch of angry female rhetoric I could care less about. She stated that Jasmine was talking to her ex. She was too needy, and she owes her money. It was never-ending. What really pops Bubble bubbles was that Jasmine was posting a petty picture with bubbles freshly Ex on the snap chat, oooooooooooh it set her off. She wanted to beat Jasmine's ass, but she decided she was just gone fly to Detroit and come fuck me was a better game plan. I can assure you I had no problem with that plan, I mean, I wasn't paying for the plane ticket, but I can pick her up from the airport and take her back, lol. This rearrangement was not my revenge; it was Bubbles. But a part of me felt satisfied. I had sex with both her close friends to make me feel better about her; having sex with my man's made me feel like I loved the girl. She had me acting entirely out of character. It was unlike me to be this pressed about someone who was not checking for me in the first place. Jasmine never found out about bubbles. And I was glad because after Jessica's fiasco, she wanted to have sex with me again, and this time I did not disappoint. That lead to us being regular sex buddies. Knowing Jasmine as I do, I Knew fucking one of her friends would lead to this. The female ego can sometimes be just as prideful as the men. I didn't know I was this manipulative. Fuck it, that sweet Derick ship sailed centuries ago. But even though I was having the time of my life, I was feeling alone.

"Alone" (age 22)

"Unreplied text messages, the constant tone of leave a message after the beep, social media posts after the read receipts are activated, favors of money, sex & advice are the only time your notification screen appears; you're alone. Don't matter how many empty condom wrappers you have on the side of the bed won't change the fact that you're still alone. Laying under your arms but still feeling ghostly because even tho your bodies are physically touching, your spirits couldn't be any further apart. You are floating through life wondering when someone will look up at you like You have just seen

*each other for the first time on your wedding day? Focusing on money
& a better life is never a bad thing, but what will it be for if you have no
one to share it with. Is the person you meet when you are successful
truly there for you? Wouldn't you rather have someone that stuck by
you even when you were catching the bus to work? Still, the feeling of
loneliness settles in Because you don't know who really loves you for
real. Not everyone will find true love in this world, but hold on to it if
you're one of the lucky ones. And never let it go because it may never
find its way back around. & you'll just end up being another floating
spirit walking through people and reaching out just to get back a
handful of air, trying to escape the inevitable emotions of being alone."*

I was in-between relations but really wanted a relationship, but
every girl I ran into end up being the same go-around. The only thing
that kept me around was good sex. And that's what Jasmine and I
had, but I wanted more out of her than she was willing to give. I
lowkey wanted to save her from her failures in men. I could have been
hers. Jasmine had me lock up; all she had to do is take advantage
and realize the guy she's looking for is right there in her face. I would
have done anything for her, but she couldn't help but look at me like
someone she can always run back to after a nigga fuck her over. I
knew my worth, and I wasn't going to continue to let her use me. So I
seek a relationship beyond her, and I got my wish, no more second
place.

"Second place" (age 23)

"How long did you think I would wait? Watching you choose other men over me is kind of like looking at an empty dinner plate. You're a fake. You tell me you love me, but your words are full of hot air balloons & I've figured you out.* grabs safety pin, deflate. I found somebody else; you're the next 225. Missed one next 15 one coming, you're late. You were my love, my moon to my night, my *I'm bout to pull up let's go somewhere, *my Alright, but you made me feel so low, but bae?....... Well, she makes me feel like I no longer want to be solo. She makes me feel like I want to be the perfect guy. I feel alive; you couldn't appreciate the boy I was, but you love the man I'm becoming. Shawty sees the boy in me & still wants me to be her man she sees coming. Ima loving, caring person that loves hard but fights most challenging for the people I love. But it's never reciprocated. All the years I dedicated to love someone who loves me as much as a paycheck & if you think that's love, baby, that's where you fuck up at. I'm the man that you're going to look back on like damn, and I had that? Why didn't he treat me like that? Maybe because you never gave me a chance, yet baby girl over here the realist, she's my second chance my first place, she's winning the race, but for you? You were this close, for you? Second place."

Chapter 6

The awakening

I'm probably the worst at cutting off people. I could never find the right words to use. I once told this girl I couldn't see her anymore because she had a kid. Fuck up, right? It was honest, but I should have delivered that better. I was indecisive and afraid to fall in love. My impulse was to reject love, and It didn't deserve me. I am also highly shallow. I stop having relations with this girl because her voice was undeniably annoying. My love life was spiraling out of control. I needed a change of lifestyle.

At the beginning of 2016, I wanted to make a change. I had got baptized in the name of Jesus. I wanted a fresh start. I wanted to leave fuck boy Derick in the past. I was ready to be in another serious relationship. I cut almost all my flings off. I even became celibate for a few months. I went on several dates but had no luck. I had my best friend hook me up with one of her friends. I wanted someone Gemini felt was of her caliber. I secretly always wanted someone identical to Gemini. Shay was the friend she decided was the girl that fit best with my personality., I had seen her once at a party downtown on New Year's Eve. Gemini was in the city, and she invited me. She was drunk af, stumbling, slurring, the usual when we link up. It was a relaxed laid-back environment. I didn't know that many people there, so I just took a seat and grabbed a drink. Moments later, here comes a drunk Gemini sitting on my lap. She had people asking if we were a couple and whatnot, but in reality, she was just using me, so she didn't get hit on. It was to the point where she got up to dance, and niggas asked me if it was cool to dance with her, "I'm like bruh you blocking lol" so after I made her get up off me, I notice her friend Shay standing in the corner, ass phattest, chocolate I wanted a bite. I Ask Gemini to hook me up, and she did.

After that party, Shay and I started to talk & FaceTime heavy, I liked her. I didn't see us being in a relationship, but she was refreshingly lovely and sweet. A few weeks later, I planned a visit up to big rapids to see her. It works out perfectly because I got to see my best friend at the same time! She was currently dating this dude that had her "dickmitized." It was unlike her to be stuck on the wrong dude for the amount of time she was, so I had to meet this man.

"Dickmatized" (age23)

-The feeling of losing control of one's self due to excellent male penetration to the vaginal wall

A wall that's built to keep out the bad & only supposed to open for Prince Charming. Not any Nigga that seems charming, letting him unlock your code & he won't even let you unlock his phone, but you'll get on the phone call him up to let him penetrate then he skates & for a while you cool with that, not knowing you keep letting him stroke you gone get used to that. Still, you just want to have fun. Who got time for that? You keep telling yourself it's just sex, but that's not how yo body act, your body craving those lips that touch, that rush you get when he thrust, pounce, and crush that wall that was meant to keep this from happening. Still, it's too late, now you're Dickmatized, and there's no escaping, you want to cut him off, but every time you try, he pops up, and you get to caving, you have no real reason to cut him off, yea he's miss behaving but y'all not together sooooo, your heart gets to racing because he's in the fast lane. You don't want to interrupt to keep the lanes from changing, you want to stay in your lane, but this dick is driving you crazy!!! You once had control. Now you were contemplating having his baby. Yea, I know that's crazy, but being Dickmatized by the wrong man isn't that crazy? He's Donal duck & you daisy! So who's really crazy? It's just dick baby, get back your control before your soul ends up pushing up Daisies.....

Keep your soul."

When I met the dude, he reminded me of a younger version of myself. He was full of game but lacked honesty. I knew this situationship wouldn't last long, but I owed it to her to let her play it out. I knew she deserved better, and at the moment, I didn't know I was referring to myself. Geminis value was unmatched, and everyone she felt attractive to were complete failures. I wanted to change her reality, but the moment for that to occur was premature. I had to harness my energy to save my best friend and redirect Once Gemini and her friend left, shay and I wanted to have some quality time. I wanted to get to know her as a person, but lust always seems to win when the attraction is mutual. We didn't have sex, but those kisses were rapid and came in variety. We kept that same energy all night, kissing, cuddling, just the perfect vibe. We watched Netflix and talked till we both passed out. The following day we woke up and decided to go out for breakfast before heading back to the city. Even though I didn't feel any fireworks, I enjoyed my time with shay. I haven't been on an actual date in months. It was stimulating to date again.

"Dating" (Age 23)

"ATTENTION!!, fellas....so you all don't open doors anymore?
Y'all just pull up & she hops in? Can you say whore?& where y'all
going? Let me guess, a dinner & a movie? Typical, & I bet you met her
off the net, trying to romance, are you after sex, you know...the usual?
If not, what's the catch? A date is for interaction, not casual sex. Do
you get the message? Naw y'all only message so why not take her to
a place that requires no interaction, ladies he's a distraction a man
that's all about no action, but with a plan to get some action, you let
him take you out, he tells you, "baby you can have whateva." You all
sit down. You get to eyeballing the steak but look at his face, sit, stare,
watch his reaction. He doesn't have it, so now you have to order
something else because he was looking at you like a cheap date,
Damn not even worth a steak? Cheapskate, but that's my generation
of dating. For goodness sake, dating these new niggas is like walking
on eggshells lord give me a break, a break from the Netflix & chills
dates, a break from "let's go to the bar," get you drunk & try to take
you home dates, a break from "I don't have enough can you pay for
the rest of yours" dates, it's a disgrace, who raised you? It must have
been a mistake. You're as worthless as a rock that can't skip across a

lake. No wonder why we can't stop our women from dating outside our race, it's a shortage of real men within our race, but we want to be kings? You can't be a king without a queen& what's a king without a queen? Nothing, a joke, something that's make-believe, something that's made to believe that it can rule without a queen, quality over quantity is not what you believe, ladies leave this joker alone and find you a REAL KING.💯"

After our date, we promised to meet again. I kissed her goodbye and made my way back to the city. The communication remains consistent for three more weeks. I can't lie; I was struggling with the distance even though I realized this reality initially. But I'm just dating, so if someone else caught my eye, I shouldn't feel bad. Because that's precisely what happens, I believe it was late Friday night strolling Instagram. I was sleepy, but before I fell unconscious, I felt a notification go off. I ignored it till the next day. It couldn't have been that important.

The following day arrives, and I'm feeling well endowed. It's Saturday, and the world is mine. I pick up my phone to see two notifications, pretty steep, right? The humor of being single. But anyway, it was a girl requesting to follow me & she liked one of my pictures. She was random, so I was thinking, where did she come from? I began to browse her IG account, and I noticed the girl was beautiful. I liked one of her pictures. It wasn't a recent pic. I had to let her know I saw her. Abruptly my interest started to fade when I read her bio. It said 18 or 19 graduation year. At first, I thought it was her age, but it looks like she graduated high school from her pictures. I had to get these questions out of my head. I commented on one of her posts and jokingly asked her, "I know you're not 18, right?" She responded with a laugh, corrected me, and told me that was her graduation year from college. I felt relieved, but I guess the conversation was more extended than she would like under her comments, so she slid in my dm's. She asked me why I chose her first picture to comment on? I'm thinking either She didn't want people in her business or two she had a man. I answered curiously, "no particular reason, was it an issue?" She replied, "no" she went on a tantrum talking about her privacy and whatnot. She also proceeds to inquire about my personal life and how attractive I was. I followed suit, and I felt like we hit it off instantly. Our first real conversation was FaceTime. I had to make sure she wasn't a catfish. Crystal was her name btw. She had a beautiful face, and she was thick, just the way I like it. I found myself talking to her more than Shay. I could be on the phone with Shay, then crystal calls, and I'll find some excuse to switch calls. I felt guilty because I talked to Shay first, but my attention was being pulled in another direction spiritually. After a few weeks, I had to stop the back and forth and make a choice. Little did I know Shay was on her way to the city to surprise me with a date. She called me to ask me what I was doing, and I was free to hang. She lived 4 hours away, so I didn't think she meant she was coming to see me. But I told her I was free, "why do you ask that"? She tells me she's in the city and what's a good place for us to eat. I was shocked and thrilled at the same time. It was morning time, and I was in the mood for breakfast, so I chose IHOP. It was in the area, and it was reasonable. She was good with the choice I picked, and we decided we were going to meet there. When she pulled up, I was lust struck. She was so delicate and delicious to look at. I gave her a warm hug and a soft kiss to express my gratitude. We went inside to grab a seat and placed our orders. I forgot about a crystal that quick with all the excitement, and she was blowing my phone up. It was unlike me to not text or call her back, but I was busy. During our date, Shay noticed my phone light, and I could tell she had questions. I quickly changed the subject about us. "Why did you drive down there to see me?" She replied that she was in Lansing, and she thought it would be cute to take me out on a date. I can tell she liked me, but I honestly like Chrystal more. After the date, I told Shay to come to sit with me in my car and talk a bit. As soon as we entered the car, I was drowned in kisses. Man, she had some soft lips. Suddenly my phone vibrates once again, but this time Shay has seen who it was. She didn't say anything but the atmosphere of the car changed. She became quiet and led to her leaving earlier than she wanted to. The immature version of myself would've just let it play out and run games on both, but I'm too old for that. I waited a few days before I broke the news to shay. She didn't like it of course. I told her I like two girls, and Before I could break it off, she fired first. She told me to know you just want her and told me to fuck off. I couldn't blame her anger, but I was hoping she respected my honesty even more. Respect is the bare minimum and at least owed her that.

Lies part 2 (age 23)

"*He wants to keep you around as if he needs more than one woman to help him stand up, boy man up. You treated women like they are as easy as drinking a glass of water (thirsty) but get mad when you can't layup. you can't always have your cake & eat it too. & you can't get mad when you get sick for overeating junk food. You don't have to play these childish games, be a man & let her know the game, give her an option to sustain, rearrange or run away. Either way, she keeps her peace of mind so she won't drive you insane. Cause once she's insane, she can damage your membrane & she can drive you so crazy you might wanna pull the mag out on your brain. It all could be prevented if you weren't trying to run the game. Don't spoon-feed her a bunch of lies so you can smack & treat her like the next thang. Why are you keeping her around? She's a good girl & you're a savage. Have you no shame? All these trains tracks around*

you, but you wanna keep her around like Thomas the choo-choo train,
"I think I can I think I can" How about you tell the truth instead of
making her think SHE CAN make you her man. How hard is it to say,
"I'm talking to other people right now, I'm single, I'm weighing my
option, but also I still wanna have fun? Are you cool with that? & if she
rejects, let her catch her flight & chose whoever next? At least you
keep your respect. Once you learn the game of telling the truth, you
will no longer need to keep her around. She'll just come around & you
get rounds without having to buy rounds, then after that, you won't
ever have to look back because she's ALL Aboard on the train tracks
without you even having to lay down a track. Man, I'm just stating
facts. 💯

Before crystal and I started, I told her upfront I was talking to someone, but it wasn't serious. So, when I texted her that she was the only one that had my attention, she believed me. I express to her that when A man knows what he wants, he goes for it. I'm no longer talking to Shay; you're the women I wanted to dedicate all my time to. She was taken back by how honest I was, and everything seems to fall right in place from there. I felt a relationship vibe with her. From my experience, I wanted to go through the seasons with her before I gave our situation a title. I wanted my next girlfriend to be my last. For the most part, she agreed to the terms, but I could tell she was young and ready to explore. The only deal breaker I let slide on her I had in the beginning was her age. She just turned 20 before we started talking. That should have been a deal-breaker, but she displayed such maturity for her age I decided to give her a chance.

47

Crystal and I dated for about two months ruffly before we made it official. I know there isn't a time frame between dating and relationships, but I wanted to wait a bit longer. I never was the guy to get into relationships because of temporary, seasonal emotions quickly. I did it for crystal, I can tell she liked me, and since we were already having consistent sex by now, she felt even more entitled to the title. But that was my first mistake; I didn't start the relationship because of my emotions. I ignored my intuition to try something new. I convince my psyche that my failed attempts at love were because I didn't take chances. Everything had to be the perfect setup to my liking. In today's world, I would call that not settling. But three years ago, I called it fate. We started from the dm's to a relationship; I guess that's how modern relationships form, right? In the beginning, I can admit I struggled mentally with being in relationship form. I was single for two years. I still had flings texting my phone and via social media. I still had soul ties I haven't broken yet. But I was true; I eventually shut it all down. I even gave Jasmine fine ass her walking papers. I can promise you she wasn't happy, but I had to uproot everything if I wanted to have a fresh foundation. In addition, Crystal wasn't thrilled with female best friends either, so every girl I had sexual relations with I had to get rid of. Which was understandable, but I also feel if you trust me, old counts shouldn't matter. I made many alterations to please crystal. Since the relationship was going so well, I have seen no need not to accolade her wishes. She quickly became my mother's favorite, and everyone in my circle and social media approved. I posted her on my Facebook; that's when you know it's real in my case. I never posted a girl on my Facebook. My family is vicious with their inappropriate comments, but my family was pleasantly friendly to Crystal which was a first for me. On the other side of the fence, Crystal's mother was on the fence about me, and her sister was basically on top of the dense, staring me down like a hawk. The only person that embraced me was her grandma. She just knew I was the perfect man for her grandbaby. She never missed a moment to tell me how handsome I was. I don't think her dog ever liked me. Bud bark at me every time was over; I think he could sense the fuck boy in my system. Ladies, listen to your dog, just like babies that can feel vibes.

The summer was coming to an end; it was the best summer I had in a long time. We went on many dates, late-night car conversations, the passion!! I felt like I was in love. This 20-year-old had me whipped. That is till she left for college. I knew deep in my heart I wasn't going to handle distance well, but I couldn't form my lips to speak my truths. I told her we would get through it, and I'll visit her as much as possible. She was only an hour away but making that drive every weekend wasn't happening. We cried together actually before she departed; our emotions were moving at lightning speed. We spent every day together from February to September, then suddenly adding distance between us was overwhelming. I got used to the consistent comfort and the lustful feelings I had when we were together. I wanted her to please me through the phone, but our levels of nasty were on two completely different levels. I was asking her to do things she's never done before or even comfortable doing. I tried to consider her age and the lack of experience she had, but I still became frustrated. I wanted her in ways she wasn't able to offer. At the same time, Jasmine used to post thirst traps when I was my most vulnerable. The day she texted me, I blocked her. I wanted to do right by crystal. She didn't deserve to be disrespected. But I had needs, and they weren't being met, so I eventually unblocked her and texted her back. The conversation was platonic at; first we did a lot of catching up over the several months we've been out of touch. We were becoming friends again. I can sense my attention was left off of crystal, so I planned a surprise visit. I didn't want to cheat on her; I had to see my baby. I needed to feel what I would be losing if I ever lost her. Before I surprised her, I quickly deleted all evidence of Jasmine and blocked her for the weekend. Even though we weren't doing anything, I still felt guilty, and I also didn't need crystal tripping over me texting her. Ever since she left for school, we started to argue over small things. Which leads to

49

hours or even days without talking to each other. It was petty, and I hated how constant it was getting. Also, another reason why I made this trip, we needed a recharge. When I did my pop up, surprised, she cried. I was so happy to see her. We spent the whole day together just walking around campus, meeting her friends, and eating out. The visit was much needed; then we headed back to her door room. I immediately remember why I didn't visit as much; her sister was her roommate. She also didn't feel like she had to leave due to her sister's company. That immediately killed my vibe. I also considered I didn't give her or her sister any heads up, but still. We ended up sitting in the lobby watching a movie under the blankets. I wanted to fuck her so bad; I started undressing her under the covers. It started to get intense, so she decided to take this movie to the showers. Where we made passionate, aggressive, soul snatching sex. It gave me a flashback on our first time and how she had tears in her eyes. I knew what sex meant to her, and I respected it. I was her best in every single category. And I didn't say that to boast. Since she was inexperienced, I explored her body in such ways she could never imagine. I gave her first orgasm, vaginal & oral. I created a monster, so now when we have sex, it's wild. We were in the shower for at least an hour or more. After the shower scene, we headed back to her room. Her sister wasn't there, so She chose to pick this time just to talk. I didn't want to any longer fight over the lengths of our daily conversation. Or how I lack sensitivity in pointless argumentative situations. I wanted to communicate openly. The first question she asked was, "why don't I visit her more" I illustrated that it was because she shared a dorm room with her sister. Something told me I shouldn't have said that; she cut into me after that. It made me not want to even ask another question. I was honest, but her state of mind was as if I was making her choose between my sister or me when I wanted some privacy. I don't visit that much so when I do, we should be able to be alone. After the long talk, we eventually went to sleep together. It was wonderful. We woke up to morning sex, but it was abruptly interrupted by her sister. Piggybacking off last night's conversation, out of frustration when her sister left, I asked her why she took everything to heart? Why can't we express how we feel without you feeling attacked or and shut down. Once again, the conversation went left, and at this point, I was ready to leave. I came up here to find peace, but it wasn't fulfilling enough for me. Yes, the sex was amazing? But the deep conversations were lacking. I wanted her to be mature, I wanted to have better communication, but the more I pushed, the worse it got. Before the conversation got out of hand, I paused it and tried my best to kiss and make up so I could continue to have a good time. I found myself conforming often; it was becoming repetitive. It felt like it was either her way or argument. And the crazy part was she felt the same way about me. I couldn't wrap my mind around it.

After we kissed and made up, we sat there on the bed and ordered some food; while ordering, I received a Snapchat. It was from Jasmine. "I thought I blocked her" we're my thoughts. Luckily, I changed her name to "T"; crystal ignored it and kept ordering our food. When she hung up, she asked me who T was and told her a male friend from college. She let it go, but I wanted to see what she sent me. I went to the bathroom to check. It was a nude video telling me this is what's waiting on me back home. I couldn't believe it, well actually I could, but why now?? I finally felt myself back in awwh of my girl but here comes this delicious, chocolate temptation. I replied, "ok, I will." Stupid, why did I write that? Was I in love or lust? Why did I continue to fall for her traps? After I replied, I quickly told her, "see her when I get back; I had to go." She left me alone after that. Heading back to crystal's room, I couldn't help but think that I just put myself In a situation I might not be able to escape from. "All males aren't men," I say that to say I still had some evolving to do. I was stuck in between staying committed but I'm in my 20's, and I'm not married. Crystal and I promised each other that we would stay faithful, and if one of us weren't feeling it anymore, we would be honest enough to say so. But guilt had my tongue; I couldn't piece my thoughts together to tell crystal how I felt. I also felt what I was going through mentally was expected; you should fulfill all of your sexual deviant behavior with your

51

partner. If not, you're guaranteed to cheat. Our communication wasn't mature enough to handle that level of subjectivity and truth. Needless to say, as soon as I left crystal, I took a sin bath in Jasmine's aroma. Both women made me whole, Jasmine satisfied my sexual deviants and gave me peace, and crystal satisfied everything in between. Jasmine became a weekly affair; it was the opposite of the weekend song; I was with Jasmine every day, and I saw my girl on the weekends. It didn't stop there, it was a few others, but the roles they played weren't significant enough for much detail. I was living a single life while crystal was in school. And when she came back home, everything went back to normal. I didn't even crave the single lifestyle while I was in her presence. I over supplemented with gifts to hide my guilt. I even had thoughts of buying her a car, glad my best friend talked me out of that one.

I felt our relationship slipping right through my fingers; I began to get sloppy. I forgot to delete message threads, call logs, and social media cookies. Cheating is another full-time job; you have to be committed. Within that moment, I realized I was more committed to hiding the truth than actually being truthful. I broke my own heart because I was morally irresponsible to my standards. The week before finals, I visited crystal once again, but this time to break it off, it was time. But on the way up there, I suddenly had a change of heart. I wanted her to be successful with her finals. I didn't want anything clouding her mind when she was trying to study. I felt I owed her that. Somehow I had to come up with something important to talk about because I told her I was coming to visit to have this "oh so important talk." But I couldn't think of anything, so I figured sex would be a better alternative.

After our session, she was emotionally hungry. She could feel my vibes were off and began to ask a million questions. I had to starve her out, I couldn't begin to engage fully, or I would have revealed my valid reason for this visit. I knew my answer was subpar, but I had to see this through. We ended the night with another argument, unfortunately. It felt like a breakup without the rhetoric; we were disconnected in every aspect of a functional relationship. And with me not being emotionally attached enough, I couldn't fix this.

After her finals (which she did great on, by the way), she was home for the summer. I chose this moment to end it. I text her to come outside to have an important talk. When she got in the car, I can tell she already knew what was about to happen. The conversation went a little something like this…….

The break up (age 25)

"We didn't work because you didn't understand me, I knew what I was getting myself into by seeing someone younger, but my mindset was, "I wanted something Fresh," somebody completely off the radar. I want to help build and shape somebody to love me like I wanted to be love because I wasn't having the best of luck in that department! So, you came around & you were everything I wanted at the time. You had one year under your belt in college, so you had a minimum experience, so on paper, everything checks out. Then we started dating; we were both very clear on what we wanted and agreed not to waste each other time. I have a one-year rule; I want to date throughout the seasons to see if you were someone I wanted to be with long term. People change like the seasons, so I wanted to adapt

& I wanted you to Adapt to me during that period. 1st mistake; I went against that, I let you pressure me into a relationship I wasn't ready for, but I said fuck it, why not? Let me step out of my comfort zone because I don't want to miss out on a potential blessing. The relationship was cool the first six months, but then you went off to school. I told myself I would be ok with the distance, but I wasn't. I struggle to stay occupied; I couldn't see you as often as I wanted, so it ate at me. After a while, the girls in my dm's started looking like a snack I could chew on till you got back in the city, but I resisted. I got back focused and continue to love you. Then Little important things started to pile up; you never understood when I was playing or when I was joking, you constantly questioned me like I was just a rookie at this relationship shit, you didn't listen to me when I talked. I always upset you with the smallest things, like taking too long to call you back. Now you're mad at me for the rest of the night. continuing to be mad about something that we could easily talk about, but you were young & naive, but all those were fixable things &, for the most part, were corrected. Then you became unappreciative at times, for example, the Apple Watch I spent 609 for, and you broke it in 3 months, then told me you didn't ask for me to buy it, then got the nerve to get mad at me for being mad that You broke it! You apologize later and try to correct it but the damage was already done...every time I mention what I had bought you, you always threw in my face that you didn't ask for it ... I wanted to make you greater but you fought me every step of the way like you didn't need me ... you were

54

so independent you could do everything by yourself to the point I use to say you need to date a beta male, you can't handle my alpha male aggression, you combated with me about everything I was losing the peace I thought I had within you and started to seek it in other places ... I needed a get away from you when you was supposed to be my get away from the world , it broke me because I wanted to be in love with you and just give you everything in me, I wanted to be vulnerable to the point where I could express anything to you , but every time I did you shut me down without even realizing and when I try to explain your actions you took offense to it & flipped it to where you was the one being victimized , it was nerve racking I smoke every chance I got because of you, I started to get migraines .. you was stressing me out and you didn't even know it , our perfect relationship everyone thought we had was crumbling every day, i loved you so much I had to make a decision to part ways before I damage you, each day got easier & easier not to talk to you, not to care about your feelings and you don't deserve that & the old me would of strung you along until you hated me, but I had to quit lying to myself telling myself that this was working when it wasn't , it's nothing we could of did to fix it , I was an asshole, I was mean, I had controlling aspects about myself, I couldn't cater to your insecurities , you was fine af why did you have insecurities???dating you was like dating my sister , and I couldn't take it , I couldn't handle your level of maturity & you wasn't ready to grow out of it yet, I wanted to grow together but I need someone on my level then we can grow together ...dating you I realize what I really *wanted! It hurt because I was disappointed that we didn't work. I brought you around my family and posted you on Facebook with all these love quotes because I just knew I found my wife. but I'm glad I found out it wasn't meant to be sooner than later; maybe four years later, we could have been something, but right now, I couldn't build you up anymore. so, when people ask me why we break up, this is why.."*

After the conversation, we didn't talk for about a month. Within that month, I was quietly debating to myself, was this the right move? I was free, but I felt I left so much on the table. It weighed me down. I had friends that lived across the street from her, and they had invited me over. In the back of my head, I knew it wasn't a good idea. The odds of us running into each other were about 100%. I decided to go anyway in hopes of clearing the air from my guilty conscience. It was around 3 o'clock when I showed up. The smell of fresh meat on the grill and kids' laughter greeted me when I entered the backyard. I was annoyed that my female friends stayed friends with the girl I recently broke up with, but I guess I will have to get over it for the day. In the midst of body slamming my nephews in the pool, I saw crystal in the corner of my eye. I was surprisingly happy to see her. I can tell she was, too, because as soon as everyone went into the house, she walked up to me and hugged me. She also noticed my tattoo on my chest and wanted to see it. So, I took off my shirt, and she began to touch it. The sexual attraction never left. I envisioned myself taking her down right there, but I had to snap out of it. Feelings were still there, But I couldn't cave. I spent the rest of the day avoiding being alone with her. I was doing great till nightfall. I've gotten too wasted, and I was too impaired to drive home. My friends suggested I spend the night. I hesitated because I had to get up early in the morning to go to work. And crystal never left, and I hopefully feared she would take advantage of me. We ended up cuddling, and I passed out before I could remember another thought. When I woke up with her in my arms, I was amazed. How could a relationship with so much potential crash and burn the way it did? She must have felt me staring at her, and she began to wake up as well. We kissed, long and passionate like it was the last kiss we would ever have. We continued to text for about a week afterward, trying to be friends. But I felt like I was giving her false hope of a situation that was never going to rekindle. I officially ended AGAIN. That was the last time that I would hear from crystal.

#Forget (age 25)

"*Your smell in my bed sheets, your presence is still felt when I lay my head down trying to get some sleep. Why do I still feel you next to me? I want to forget, but you meant that much to me. It's not a quick fix; you were supposed to be my wife to be? Why did you leave me? Why did you let me let you go mentally? Why couldn't you be the girl that was meant for me? I thought I found the right one, but now your just another one that had potential through the roof but fail miserably, I gave you a piece of me, being with you was like a puzzle, we started off good but somewhere during the middle the pieces wasn't fitting equally, I hate to treat you like you wasn't shit to me, but that's the only way I know how to keep my sanity, I let you go peacefully , now I'm wondering around the streets trying to not let my thoughts get to me , this girl right here a freak & she's looking like she wants a piece of me... but I'm good on that piece of meat , I need something whole, Issa snack won't fuel my soul mentality, spiritually or physically .. you wouldn't be any good for me, I'll use & abuse you like you'll the next 15 one coming ....like Rosa parks it's history, I still love you but I'm trying to remove that viciously, I finally deleted all our pictures from my memory, it was really hard to let you go but you didn't even wish me a Happy Birthday, yeaaaaa that was it for me, you don't even know what that did to me, put me in my feelings & made me delete our thread, our last bit of history forget trying rekindle our chemistry, I only get like this when I'm alone in the dark"*

Chapter 7
Perfect Mix

"New beginning" (age 26)

"How did I get to this point again? I thought I was free of this feeling of feeling alone. Even when I was in a relationship, there were days where I felt my love wasn't there; I poured so much into her but left me half empty. Will I ever feel like I can't live without you? Why is it so easy for me to replace you? I just want you in the race, but you're so far behind I can't reach back, I won't reach back, risking second place. Others are trying to join the race because I'm single, but I don't want a date, & the one I had one-night stands with wanna date, I can't catch a break. I feel

Like I'm drowning in my sauce with no hope of finding my true soulmate. I'm around beautiful women every day, but it's a temporary reliever for what I truly want. Being looked at as the forbidden fruit, what's the point of having the juice when all she's going to do is drink & never replenish, nerve finish, but expect me to not look at the cup half empty. I'm in another dimension wishing upon a star for a happy ending that seems light-years away. I'm back in the beginning, and the black board wiped off. I thought I was finished. I thought I solved the equation, but all I did was become someone else's lesson, man. That's hard to replenish; I was born a winner, but yet I'm not winning! I

want to need you more than you need me, but you end up playing
second fiddle to my other dimension & I know that sickening, but what
you expect me to do when the lord & savior whispers in your & tell
you, you're not finished. she's not the one, grab ink to the eraser
board & start again; a new beginning. "

It is a smooth 78 degrees, and the sun just went down. There was a slight breeze without a single cloud in the sky. It felt amazing, I was single, and I was happy about it. I had to start living for myself, and that's precisely what I did.

It's the beginning of June, and I'm ready to act out. My friend Lia (a mutual friend of Gemini and I) wanted to hang out. Lia was chocolate and thick in all the right areas, so when she hit me up to hang, I'm not going to lie; I had all evil intentions. I wanted to ruin her life in a fun sexual way. When we met up, she had a friend with her who was also a nice small-framed, snack. We started the day with drinks and laughter. The more drinks that enter my system, the more I knew I would take Lia home tonight. I remind you we've been great friends for years, but today she was in my path. As the sun touched the horizon, I told the ladies I was having fun, but I was getting ready to leave. Lia rode with her friend, but she asked me if I could take her home; instead, I agreed. I parked in the Greektown parking lot. It was a long walk, but she was willing to walk with me. Luckily her friend decided to give us a lift to my car. When we got to my car, I ask Lia straight up did she want to have sex, and she was taken back at first. Then I kissed her, and she began to open up.

"In the parking lot of the casino, though?' she uttered. Well, that's what the tinted windows are for, I replied. I guess that was sufficient for her because we continued. Then we stop briefly; what's wrong, I asked? Where's your condom she replied? Myself, I was looking puzzled because I haven't used one in so long, I didn't even think to carry one. I told her I didn't have one, and just like a booty call scene, I had to run to get one. I was so mad, but I had to do what I had to. It took me about 15 minutes to find the liquor store. The whole way back, I was praying she wasn't asleep. Luckily when I came back, she was ready. I gave her rounds in that parking lot; it was terrific. But the parking lot started to become crowded, so we figured it was our time to exit. On my way to her house, I was daydreaming about more rounds. She must have read my mind because as soon as we pulled into her parking lot, we went right back at it. During this time around, she asked me the sprung question, "why are you doing this to me? I replied with a smirk, "because your sex is fire. I should have stopped, but I continued till she tapped. I felt replenished; I was ready to make her my sneaky link for the rest of the summer. Once we were finished, she told me she would hit me up tomorrow and have a good night. I told her I would and watched her till she made it into the house safely. I never told her this, but I didn't go home right away. I fell asleep right there in the parking lot. The alcohol mix with all of that sex I couldn't drive home. I spent the night in the car, and when I awoke in the morning, I drove home.

When I woke up that next day, I told Gemini what happened and she couldn't believe it. I told her I thought I messed up my friendship with Lia, and she inquired why. I think I gave her too many rounds, I replied. She laughs and continues to assure me that everything is going to be okay. Man was she wrong, It was our birthday month Gemini, Ashley, and I celebrated our June birthdays together all of June. This year we went to an event called trap karaoke. It's a large venue full of people doing karaoke to their favorite rap song. Before the event, we all got a hotel room to pregame, etc. Lia had ended up showing up to the room to drink and turn up.

After our last session, Lia started to act noticeably awkward around me. At the time, I didn't know that she was probably in her feelings. Either about the sex or that I was hung up on another girl in the room. She wasn't rocking with it either way, but I made it my mission to find out. I asked Lia did she want to come to the liquor store with me, and she agreed. On the way there, I wanted to make sure we were cool, and she waved me off like everything was fine and to not worry about her. I felt better after the conversation, but I also suggested we shouldn't have sex again either. I did not want to ruin our friendship; I valued her too much. She agreed to my terms. We made it back to the room to begin the pregame. Lia left shortly after the turn-up. It was a room full of ladies, and I was right in the middle, which was usual for me.

Gemini has always been my best wingman, and I love her for that.

Trap karaoke was about to start, and ladies were almost done getting ready. I felt this night was going to be eventful. The place was packed and full of energy. We partied to our favorite songs; they Heard some spoken words and good throwback jams. Everyone had a good time, but we were all sober, so it was time to go. We were going to head back to the room to finish out the night. Feeling nice and on tip, I decided to share the bed with another one of Gemini friends. I had my eyes on her the whole night. Her name was Kiara, and I can tell that Kiara was feeling me as well. We had a profound spiritual vibe I couldn't quite understand, but I felt it. If she allowed me, I would have had sex with her right there in front of Gemini. I knew Gemini wouldn't have cared anyway, and we're best friends; this what we do. But instead, we just kissed and cuddled all night. I felt terrible that it was Gemini birthday and I was getting all the action right next to her.

62

In the morning, we all decided to get some brunch at this low-key spot called a toast. We had everything from Mamosa's to whatever you could fit in your mouth. I decided to be friendly and pay for everyone's meal. It was the gentleman's thing to do. After brunch, the ladies were going to head back to the room because later on they were going on a party bus. I passed on that I wasn't feeling it. But that also left the room to myself, I could have called someone to slide through, but I already had my eyes locked on Kiara. I just drank by myself, ordered some food, and stayed put till she returned.

I didn't intentionally target Gemini friends, but I was always around, and now that I'm single, everyone is fair game. After that weekend, Kiara and I continued talking and Facetime. she had this womanly essence about her I never felt before. We ended up connecting the following weekend again for Ashley and I Birthday party. Ashley threw a house party, and everyone came. Forgive me for not remembering the entire night. I died for some time and was brought back to life. I'll explain in more detail later.

I remember talking to an old friend about the party tonight, and she asked me if she could tag along. Forgetting that Kiara and LIA were going to be there, I told Reasha , okay. I proceeded to pull up, and when she entered the car, she gave me flashbacks of how we used to be. She was the reason why I knew how evil women could be. Y'all wanna hear the story? Bet because I was going to say that shit anyway.

It was a regular day, well at least at first. I hit Resha up to see if she wanted to have a session and just vibe, she agreed. I told her I would pull up around 8pm, she told me to grab a bottle; she was trying to have a wild night. She had no Idea the foreshadowing manifesting she was conjuring. About three hours later I pulled up and she was basically naked at the door waiting on me. I felt the lust energy consume me like venom attaching to spiderman. I was in the sunken place, watching my higher self-take the back seat to my ego. With each stroke I felt a piece of myself leaving and another energy reattaching. Rounds after rounds, climax after climax the vibrations were so high, we both passed out in each other's aura. Moments later we heard a bang at a door. Resha jumped up like she recognized the energy. I put on my clothes and so did she. Then we heard another bang, this time the guy shouted " Resha open this damn door" It was her baby daddy she told me. In my head I'm thinking, "Now I gotta scrap with her baby daddy, great. After that thought she told me to act like her cousin. Your cousin? I asked in curiosity. Lowkey I never told her this but I was excited to show my acting skills. I randomly think about what I would do If i was in a situation like this and now it's my time to shine. At least I didn't have to act like a gay best friend. Nervously Resha opened the door. He came in asking "whose car is that in the driveway and where is my son?" I came out of the kitchen with little man like chill bro its mine, I'm Resha's cousin Nate. He looked at me funny at first then he gave me a dap and apologized for coming in the house on tip (Hostility). Once Resha realized her plan might work, she started to relax. So now we decide to all sit in the living room. I'm playing with Reshas son like he's, my nephew. Play fighting and just doing the most. Meanwhile Resha and her baby daddy were having a conversation across the room. It started off hostile then he started to cry. I'm thinking, this situation is wild. And to make matters worse the guy asked me for some advice on their situation. I wanted to be like dude I'm not her cousin I'm just the comfort Dick. But I cared for Resha and I didn't want to blow her cover. I continued to play my role till he left. I couldn't believe he bought that act. It fucked with me for a while after that. If she could do that to the person, she had a child with then I didn't stand a chance. I slowly started to separate myself from her. Still very much attached to the sex all I can say, it was a soul-snatching experience; stay away!! Still Thinking to myself, even after everything we've been through, I was hoping she still had a vibe for me, but I'll just see how this night plays out.

I say we pulled up at the party around nine, and the house was already packed with people. I can see what kind of night this was going to be already. I text my man's Lance to come through just In case a situation escalated or I simply passed out and needed someone to carry me. Passing around hugs and handshakes through the crowd, I made my way downstairs where the birthday girl and my best friend were. Immediately as I made it down the stairs, I saw LIA and Kiara next to each other, talking as I walked through with this girl neither one of them had ever seen before. Kiara was unbothered, but I couldn't say the same about LIA even though she had brought a date as well. We all Mixed and mingled, conversations filled with light humor chased with a touch of sarcasm.

According to a few reliable sources, I had reached my maximum alcohol consumption and passed out on the couch. Kiara noticed me and proceeded to take me upstairs. All I remember was throwing up all over the floor. I was thinking to myself (why do I always do this shit). That pretty much ruined any moment I thought I was about to have. I blackout again; the next thing I remember is being submerged in water. Before I passed out, my cousins wanted to come to the party, and I had sent my location to them. But that was hours ago. I didn't think they would show up.

Gemini proceeded to tell me what I felt was an exaggerated story about how my cousins rushed in. She described it as a scene in power. They came in and demanded to know my whereabouts. They maliciously ran up the stairs, picked me up, took me to the bathroom, and dumped my face in the bathtub until I woke up. As you can see, I was having a swell time. Through all the commotion, I forgot about Resha (the girl I brought to the party). I found her upstairs on the couch halfway passed out smoking with my best friend. I asked her if she was ready to leave. "Yes, she responded. As she's gathering her things, I asked Lance to ride with me to take her home. I wasn't in the best condition to drive, hence why I asked Lance to drive, but he wasn't either. So, Resha ended up driving my car to her house. All thoughts of having a moment disappear; I couldn't believe she was over me. I must have done a number on her. But I enjoyed our friendship; I hugged her goodbye and watched her walk into her home. Lance still wasn't able to drive, so I had to drive us back to the party.

When we pulled back up to the party, it was still live as if we never left. I felt 100% better, so a few more shots couldn't hurt. It was my birthday, and my attitude was on fuck it!

It was birthday cake time, and Kiara decided to sing happy birthday to Ashley and me. It was beautiful; no one has ever sung happy birthday to me before (that could actually sing). As the night dwindled, Kiara and I became closer. I was too drunk to have sex, so we just cuddled in the nude. I guess you can say I had an eventful night. I was able to avoid all drama and, at the same time, live my best life. Sunlight touched the corner of my eye, waking me to the point of consciousness. Kiara's aroma was so strong and pleasant I didn't want to move a muscle. She must have felt the same because we just laid there for about an hour in silence, enjoying the moment for what it is. Gemini random obnoxious laugh ruined the transcending shared dream Kiara, and I was having. Consciously I felt Gemini felt away about Kiara and me, and I think we both felt it. Probably it's the reason why we never physically crossed that line.

The day was Sunday, and all the fun was coming to an end. The girls went back to Lansing, and life continues as scheduled. Kiara and I continue our daily talks but mainly on a spiritual level. She was exceptionally mentally stimulating, and I enjoyed the depths of our conversation. But physically, Jasmine continues to be my go-to. Her lustful aura empowers my decision-making. I felt like a sex slave, mentally drowned in her feminine energy. In the month of July, I spent almost every day with her. My mother always told me if she made my heart flutter to the point that logic doesn't exist, run far. Those words burned in the back of my memory. It was easy to confuse love and lust with Jasmine. I wanted to love her because the physicality was soulfully gravitating. I accumulated the courage AGAIN to tell Jasmine how I felt. Her response wasn't quite what I was expecting after all of this time. It was more of an "I'm still looking and If I can't find him, then sure" vibe. At that moment, I had an awakening that resembled the black panther and the lion king. How can I turn off this pain body? Why did I keep inserting my emotions into a person that only accepts them when it's convenient. At that moment, I realized what I was doing. I was emotionally detached from her. It's not easy to break an unhealthy bond; sometimes, it takes repeated heartbreak for the mind to adjust to reality finally. Jasmine showed me with her words and actions what time she was on. I thought pure love could change that. But only a fool trades love for self-respect. We still kept our friendship, but that moment was the last straw for me.

"Notice me" (Age 25)

"I remember when I held you while you had a mental breakdown, hair a mess, nose running... hysterically crying in my arms begging me never to leave you. I help you in your darkest hour even after I resented you all these years for treating me like I didn't deserve you, when in reality you didn't deserve me, chasing a beautiful devil can turn you into something you're not. You're no longer in control. She pulls the strings. "acceptance" is a real drug, and I use to abuse it. What would you do to be wanted? I loaned out my heart for temporary feelings, I slept by your doorstep waiting for you to let me in, but you never did. One day you open the door, but to let someone else in, In the morning you open the door, let him out, but gave me a blanket and some food, and I accept that. I didn't understand why you didn't think karma would pay you back for using me as a clean doormat. No one else could rub their feet on it, but you can. That is until I remember the key was under the mat. I used it to unlock the chains you had around my heart. I broke free of this beautiful misery & when you finally decided to open the door. I won't be there; I won't continue to accompany misery."

Chapter 8
Reflection & truth

Two weeks later, I was back on the road to Lansing. Honestly, I didn't know the exact reason why, but I had a feeling it was a spare of the moment "turn up" session that might last the whole weekend. When I pulled up, Gemini friends were in full swing. Daisy and Lauren were having a twerk session, and Kiara was drunk singing karaoke. A house full of women, and I was the only masculine energy per usual (AGAIN). I blended in and enjoyed the festivities. Through the clouds of smoke and the blurred vision of alcohol, I found myself locking eyes with my best friend several times.

At the time, I couldn't tell if it was an illusion or reality, but she gave me a different vibe that day. The way she danced, the sound of her voice, the smell of her perfume turned me on in every way and intensified my urges. I remember thinking, if I get the slightest hint, I'm taking it. The turn up lasted for a few more hours; then daisy alerted us that a new episode of Insecure was on. It turned into a mad scramble to the bedroom to get a good spot. I made sure I sat next to Gemini, But Daisy also sat next to me. At this point, I honestly didn't know who I wanted to pursue. I knew Gemini still had me in the friend zone, so my flirting with Daisy shouldn't have bothered her, right? I was absolutely wrong, Gemini didn't say anything, but I felt her energy of disapproval. And to prove her disapproval, she grabbed my dick in the middle of us laying there watching tv. Then she quickly let it go. I took it as a sign and rolled with it. Moments later, I found my hands gripping her ass, and I felt a booty massage would spark the mood. She also had on a dress that was so tight the vibrations of the massage exposed her bare rear. At this point, I was at a point of no return. I put my hands on her naked flesh and started to grip every inch of her firmly.

Before I got into too much of a grove, I looked around to make sure I wasn't being watched, and to my surprise, everyone was asleep. That gave me free rein to get more aggressive with my touches. I felt her feminine energy pass through my fingers like an electric current. She was softer than a bare, fathered pillow. I rode the sexual pulse till she climaxed, and I made her cum from a simple booty massage. The lines have been crossed, and now it's time to take possession of what I've always wanted. I must put out a disclaimer: I froze up when it was time to clash souls. She got up from the bed and signaled for me to go to the other room. I just sat there for a min to gather my thoughts. Like this is happening? and we were both sober?? "The girl of my dreams is now a reality, and I must seize the moment." Those were my thoughts, but my body was stuck to the bed. I had to smack myself to snap out of it. I followed Gemini to the bedroom, where she was fully naked ready for me to penetrate her like a drill to a screw. She smelled like fresh lake water with a scent of cinnamon. I entered her and immediately knew where I belonged. I might sound crazy, but our whole future together flashed before my eyes. I was already in love, and now I'm over the hill. I started to have an out-of-body experience. My consciousness split in two. I thought of having a baby on one shoulder and the second shoulder I never felt comfortable enough with a woman to want to create life with until now. And before I knew it, I was Cumming inside her with no warning.

After I ejaculated, I came back to earth, and once I realized what I did, I couldn't believe it. I quickly became silent, and Gemini noticed. She asked me if I just faked an orgasm. Caught off guard by the question, I laughed awkwardly and told her no. Then I said in a low tone, "I didn't pull out." She asked me to repeat myself, "I came in you," and as soon as she caught wind of what I was saying, she started to hit me, playfully but not really. I could tell she was shell shocked at just what happened.

Not only are we hooking up soberly, but I potentially just got her pregnant. It was awkward silent energy afterward. I moved to the other side of the bed, and we didn't say anything for at least 20 minutes. I immediately knew she was pregnant; I felt it once my sperm left the sack. I was terrified for the future. What If she didn't want to keep it? What if she didn't want to be a family? We were just friends up until this point. Where do we go from here? I needed reassurance, but I knew it wasn't the right time, so we just sat till someone broke the silence. I'll never forget it. Her exact words were, "well, I'm still horny." I responded by saying that was the best sex of my life; if you are pregnant at this point, it is what it is. She agreed and went back to it for round two. The sex was so rejuvenating I had to cum in her again. My pull-out game was non-existent, and I did not have a care in the world. After round two, it was still a disconnect; we still weren't vibrating on the same frequency. I was going to leave because I had to head back to the city for work, but she wanted me to spend the night, so I did.

When I returned home, I was still uneasy about our situation, but I tried to act normal when Gemini and I did talk. She called me right before I left for my trip to Caribana. We talked about her taking a pregnancy test in two weeks to confirm our suspension, but that was about it. I was avoiding her for the most part. I didn't want to go back to being friends with a baby, I wanted a family, and I wasn't sure if we were on the same page yet. I also wanted to enjoy my trip. If I were going to receive any bad news, it would have been better to hear it after the trip was how I rationalize.

Before the guy trip, I had the mindset of fucking every fine chick I seen. After last weekend all I could think about is being a father. I enjoyed myself, but I behaved myself as well. I already felt my mentality changing to family mode. Gemini was all I could think about the whole trip. Beautiful women surrounded me, and I could care less. I even FaceTime Gemini In the midst of it, she told me I didn't have to & to have a good time. I was Infatuated with the thought of creating life with the person I loved since college. She penetrated my thoughts the entirety of the trip.

Once I got back, the energy was still spotty between us. I didn't know how to overcome this awkwardness. A week goes by, and I received a text message that almost made me run my front end of my car into a light pole. It was a picture of a positive pregnancy test! I froze, like this is happening, I'm about to be a father!! Her words that followed the picture was "so you know we're definitely in a relationship, right?" And it wasn't a question, it was a clear statement, and I wanted all smoke. (I was ready to welcome any obstacles this pregnancy had Instore.) I think I called Lance and told him first, and then I texted the group chat. Everyone thought I was lying till I posted the pregnancy test! I remember vividly the group going crazy. "Your momma is about to kill you," a few congratulations, and a few "you sure it's yours." The following person I told was my father.

I decided to tell him in person; tears were his initial reaction. I thought he was angry, but he was relieved it wasn't my ex and then hugged me. I could tell he knew this time was coming

72

soon. He just didn't think this soon. Now my mother, on the other hand, her reaction surprised me. She was in all of my ex-crystal, and I could understand why; they were practically twins. They built a pretty good bond over those two years. And I think she felt that time was coming to an end. Her congratulations didn't have any exclamation points behind it. Her first words were, I knew you were cheating on crystal with her. (Completely false for the record) but that was her thought process. Hurt my feelings, but I didn't express it; it wouldn't have mattered anyway.

I believe I told a few more close friends and family members, and then I shut it down. Gemini wanted to fix our relationship, so she proposed that we have a first date to smooth things out. When I tell you that was the most awkward date of my life. The idea was for us to act like we didn't know each other and start from scratch. (Dumb, right?) that's what I thought, but I didn't have any better ideas at the time. Halfway through the first official date, we decided that we should just go back home and fuck the awkwardness away, and that's precisely what we did. It was passionate; it was, Exhilarating, it was pure love! I worshiped her body like the God she was. I was satisfied with every sexual position she could have thought of. Once we finished, we just laid there. She asked me did I still feel akw- and before she could even finish the word. I said, hell no, we are getting married, lol.

Reality sits in once the non-sound of silence appears. "I still live with my mom" "she gotta move to Detroit. I'm not raising my kid in Lansing" was my thought process. Luckily, I was going through this new lifestyle change with my best friend, so every obstacle we encountered, we hurdle it. I visited Lansing every weekend until she decided to move to the city after a few months. Still, no place she had to move in with a close friend till I handle my business. I had to get brave and find a place for my woman and child to lay their head. Another couple of months went by till I accomplished that goal, but I did it. Our first place together, and I couldn't be happier! I have to take this moment to give a special shout-out to Ashley. she did not have to open up her home to us. I will be forever grateful, and you will continue to receive life's greatest blessings for your kind spirit, thank you, and love you much!! We Cherish you forever ♥.

The sequence of having a baby is exceptionally expediting. Before our home was available to move in, we had two baby showers and a maternal baby shoot on our plate. It was bang-bang, but every event was exceptional and a success. I couldn't believe the amount of support our families showed us. We didn't have to buy diapers for the first year.

My employers at my job even got us a rocking chair with her name on it. From the hand-stitched Athena blankets, pillows, and bathrobes; to the car seats and many clothes, I was genuinely thankful.

Athena was thankful as well. In fact, she was so thankful she decided that she wanted to see everything herself. Now Gemini due date was April 21st, and she was going to the doctor for a routine check-up. The doctors decided that Athena was ready to come out today, and they were going to start inducing labor immediately. Waking up that morning, I wasn't mentally prepared to hear "get to the hospital quickly; it's happening today," which is exactly what happened when I was at work. I hung up the phone and told the fellas the situation, and I was on my way.

Once I got to the hospital, Gemini was still hoping that she didn't have to deliver today because the induction was moving slower than average. But the doctors reassure her they were going to manually break her water and get Athena out today. Three days later, it's now April

11th. Gemini wanted a natural birth, but with the induction that was no longer possible, now there were chats of C-section, which broke her heart. She never wanted that procedure, but it was now our reality. Hours later, we were preparing for surgery & Gemini was very emotional. I held her hand the entire time till it was time for us to part. I hated that she had to spend even a second without me, but when we reunited, I saw my child being pulled from her mother's stomach. Athena! My child is finally here in this world. This whole nine-month process has been leading up to this moment. I cried; I finally got to see a part of me that's still pure. As a family, we just held each other and cried a tear of happiness!! The new journey of our life begins now.

Things finally started to look bright, then another storm appeared. I lost my job, and my car went down in the same months after. Feeling less than a man, Gemini held me down, pregnant and all she got her a great job and helped support us till I could get back on my feet. I take pride in being a provider for my family, but's it's a blessing to know even at the early stages of life, she was able to help me without belittling me. This was when I knew I wanted to put a ring on her finger, and from this moment forth, I made sure those thoughts would manifest into this physical realm. I decided to flip what it seems like a loss into a win. I get to be a stay-at-home father for a while. Most fathers don't get the chance to be able to take care of their children throughout the early infant stages. It was a beautiful experience I wouldn't have traded for anything in the world.

I was still paying the rent with my unemployment, but watching Gemini help handle the household was terrific to see. But After I bounced back with a job, I wanted Gemin to quit her job and go back to being a house mom. She could work from home, go back to school, whatever she wanted. But it was a choice to work or not. I loved that dynamic, and I felt it was better for Athena; she's her first teacher. But she didn't see it that way. She felt a sense of independence and a sense of control on my part. She really wanted to say," I don't make enough to support and live comfortably." I had to eat that as a man and elevate. I had to make her feel more secure as a man; I decided to go to trade school. I wanted to give her the life I dreamed of. "To obtain what you never have, you have to do what you've never done."

Feel that (age26)

"Her heart is open, and she's annoying because she loves you. She wants to spend every second with you because you compliment her energy. Don't take this love for granted, don't get it twisted. This heart over hills queen is sharing her earthly powers with you. You made her feel comfortable enough to open up her soul. She trusts this. She can also ruin your life if you don't hold her heart dear; you're regret making her regret doing life with you. This isn't Mount Everest. You can't speed two months climbing to her heart, fighting through the cold (her pain). Fighting through the pitfalls (her trauma), fighting to maintain oxygen(her trust issues), even fighting to eat, drink and sleep, (her built up the anxiety of falling in love again) just to reach the top, stick a flag in her heart for proof you were here, and come down.
*Pause **

Feel that .....

If the plans aren't till death do us part don't part the Red Sea, don't pass go, it's plenty of women that's looking for a paid good time stop wasting someone time if the time spent isn't genuine."

Chapter 9
Best-friend

Our birthdays were approaching, and I finally figured out the perfect proposal. Instead of doing it on her birthday, I was going to do it on mine instead. She would have never thought I would make a day that's about me about her. I decided to disguise the secret proposal with a pool party. My right-hand man that held me down every step of the way was Netty & Ashley. These two made sure Gemini remained outside the box, which wasn't an easy task because she questions EVERYTHING! I ordered the ring. I had Gemini make and send out the invites. Things were going to plan until two weeks before the date the ring I ordered was only the ring mount. Who buys only the ring mount!!!!! Now it's a mad scramble to find a 1k diamond to put on this mount. Low on cash, I had to borrow from my friend Steve and netty. Netty gave her last; it was mind-blowing that she would ever do that for me. My love grew 10x for her that day, and together plus Athena went to purchase the ring! It felt like Christmas; we were so excited for this moment! The hardest part was acting normal around her. The day before the event, I made sure she got her nails done; I made sure she had her hair done and a new bathing suit. My uncle was the clutches for allowing me to use his house. I owe him big time!

The whole night I couldn't sleep; I kept dreaming about how her reaction was going to be, how will I feel in the moment? My heart rate is currently increasing, as I explain in detail. Before we left the house for the pool party, Gemini reached for my phone as I was showing my cousin the ring via picture text. She grabbed it, and I panicked and slapped the phone out of her hand. She gave me this crazy look of death, and I started praying that she didn't spaz on me. I promised you it wasn't what it looked like. I don't even remember what I said.

I think I blacked out, and she walked away. But I knew later she would completely understand, so I wasn't that worried. I remember I had to return my swim trunks that Gemini bought; they were too small. But when I walked into the store to exchange the shorts, I didn't have the receipt, and the clerk wouldn't give me my money back for these tiny trucks. I also didn't have enough time to explore any other store. I had to just take my loss and wear them. I'm not gonna lie; I felt like an NBA 70's basketball player. A few shots later, I could care less; I was on one. (Having a blast)

It's almost showtime. I'm just waiting on a few more bodies to fill in. My brother was so late to the party everyone got excited because finally, the wait was over. I had my cousin slick distract Gemini while I gathered everyone on to the grass. I had Gemini friends and family handpick roses in a heart shaped platform for Gemini and me. When I finally got everyone to where I wanted them to be, I came back and grabbed Gemini's hand and told her everyone was about to sing me happy birthday. I gave Kells the heads up, and he gave me the smoothest ring handoff in-ring history; no one even saw it. I gave another signal for everyone else to say happy birthday, then I proceeded to say......

Over these years, you've become my vise,
my natural high
My energy sources
In a world filled with black kryptonite
Our vibe is so unique
it reminds me of our relationship to the sun
Drowning in vitamin D

8 billion people In the world & you only see me
You were put on this earth to be the black goddess you are
I look at you like I'm gazing at the stars
My black Bonnie, I love how ambitious you are
You cut like a knife, but it's to remove the poison and
you heal my scars, you deserve a happy life, but these words aren't doing this justice

So Ima drop to one knee and ask you this one question.

will you marry me"

She said yesssssssss!!! And right on queue, it was raining rose petals. June 30th, 2019, we decided to do life! And it was the most significant decision of my life. I can honestly say I THINK I LOVE MY BESTFRIEND. ❤

__Chapter 10__
The audacity!?

As much as I would love to want this story to end in a happy ending, that's just not reality. "I THINK I LOVE MY BESTFRIEND "was the original title of the book. But as you can see, changes had to be made. Let's pull some layers back, shall we? Remember the beginning of Geminis and I's relationship? Both were single, both having our prior engagements that were left unresolved? We dropped everything we had going on to try to make a family work without even dating first. Never having a romantic connection, never truly building that intimate connection. Huge foundational pieces were missing from the puzzle that we tried to piece together during the relationship.

The engagement was the highlight of my life, but it was also the peak of the roller coaster. Suppose anyone knows Gemini. She's far from typical. It's like she was already in the future, and everyone is playing catch up (in relationship terms). Monogamy was never part of the equation; she felt a man should be a man and shouldn't be restricted to one woman for the rest of his life. It wasn't not logical. I know many will disagree with that thought process, but who cares. Every situation is different, and what works for you and yours, that is all you focus on. I felt that this was the perfect setup. I can have my friends with boundaries, potentially turning this situation into a poly(polygamy). For the ones who are not educated on the subject. Polygamy, by textbook definition, is "the practice of marrying multiple spouses. When a man is married to more than one wife or at the same time". Gemini also always wanted a sister wife (which also means co-wife). Scalping our ideal relationship, I thought we were on the same page, and I moved as such. For disclaimers purposes, we both weren't ready for this kind of commitment, poly or monogamy. Too many unresolved childhood traumas, no shadow work, egos undiscovered, the true identity of self-missing, and lack of maturity plague us from the start.

Jasmine was a topic of discussion, Gemini was familiar with her for obvious reasons, and she thought that would be an excellent door to open for our situation. Before contacting Jasmine, I didn't know the built-up tension she had for me. I completely disregarded all signs because of my selfish wants. The beginning meetups were relaxed, and the conversations were entertaining, but it wasn't genuine. Well, at least it didn't feel like it was on her part. Gemini wanted to figure out what she was hiding, so she allowed us to have a night alone to figure shit out. And that's exactly what needed to happen. All hell broke loose. If you never met the raw emotions of an Aries and its explosiveness. Come to find out, Jasmine didn't want a poly. She wanted me and was jealous or envious of Gemini situation. She thought Gemini stole the life she was supposed to have and hated me for it. She felt like I abandoned her to live my picture-perfect life, and she didn't want to be a tag along. Jasmine had every right to feel how she wanted to feel, but she could have let that be known for the beginning instead of putting on this facade that she was down. After the intense shouting match, she calmed down and wanted to be intimate. Gemini was aware that this was a possibility and didn't have a problem with it as long as I didn't hide anything and kept the open communication of how I felt.

After that night, it was clear that Jasmine wouldn't be a logical fit, but I still had a robust sexual soul tie that I wanted to bury. But after that night, I realize maybe it was a mistake letting Jasmine in because it won't be that easy to shut it all down. Once Gemini realized we wouldn't add her, she wanted me to cut all communications because she knew she wouldn't respect the boundaries of staying friends. I also believe a part of her didn't trust that I wouldn't cross the line. And she had every right to believe that because that's what I did. Nothing sexual, but I did still have a love for her, and I expressed that. But instead of openly expressing it to Gemini, she found out through my phone. That opened the window for her to explore her hiding feelings she had with her ex-lover. The difference between the situations was my entanglement moved out of state. Hers was less than 20 minutes away, and while mine was ending, she was just beginning. Once Gemini's feelings were activated, all the fucks that were giving were gone. She started to be sneaky and started to lie about her whereabouts. I'm trying to rebuild our trust, and she's trying to test the waters with her ex. I ignored it. I felt I deserved the disrespect because I started it. But it got worse. I remember very vividly I was at work and I got the phone call. Gemini told me she met up with her ex that day, and she told me openly she still had feelings for him and wasn't sure if she wanted to commit to me thoroughly. I can only express my feelings in a poem.

"Why" (age 28)?

"Why does the sun leave and replace his light with darkness? Why does love hurt so much that the light you give can quickly turn into darkness? What's the point of being if the only decision to make is between living a lie or dying with the truth? I can't tell you how sick I am of the abuse. If love was an arrow, I'm wearing a bulletproof. The pain must be processed, but why do I always have to process it? I'm so used to the pain I can make it my last name. I feel like a clown in this world, but instead of telling the jokes, the jokes on me. Maybe I'm too blind to see that somewhere out there is a better me. Let the light shine so I can be who I'm supposed to be, but then comes nightfall

where here lies my pain and misery, love turns from light to darkness, and I can't see."

I ended the engagement. There was no point in moving forward with a wedding if this was how she was feeling. I hated her for destroying the family I imagined us having. I guess it was only what I envision. I'm focusing on building a house from the ground up and living a happy life, and she decides that was never her truth. The whole time she felt this way, and Jasmine allowed her to live out that fantasy. In her perfect world, she wanted to have both me in her ex. To be able to love freely. At this point, I'm about ready to smack fire out those devil lips that are piercing my heart. "The audacity, I'm the one that took over all the bills and the weight to allow you to figure out what you truly wanted to do with your life. I gave you everything you wanted, but yet it wasn't good enough because you still out here searching for some bullshit ass fairy tale that will never happen. I had the perfect setup. Why? Why blow it up for a feeling? Living in your truths? Fuck your truth. The truth is I have never been loved the way that I loved. No one had ever chosen me. You were only here because we made a baby, you tried to love me, but once it got waste deep, you folded on me. What does love really mean when you give it your all, and it still fucks you over."

These raw emotions weighed on me for months, but It gets worst. I received a Facebook message from her current ex-girlfriend. That's right, he had a whole situation himself, But I'll get back to that. The message proceeded to say, "how you can try to continue a relationship with a woman that was openly kissing other men" and a whole bunch of angry rhetoric that holds no value. The actual fire under my eyes was the kissing part. I immediately called Gemini to discuss this message and to ask her was it true. She denied the allegations. In my heart, I felt she was lying, but she already told me life-altering news. Why would she lie about anything else? With that information, I responded to the girlfriend, basically protecting Gemini. I told her to get out of my messages with added drama. Gemini calls back and tells me they did kiss……………………………..

Kissing is like oral pleasure to me. It's as intimate as any sexual touch. At this point, I'm so done I can't even function. Thank God I wasn't home. I was working a long 16hr shift. Imagine trying to maintain your composure around your co-workers while you're losing your fiancé. My mind was so scrambled I just shut down. I don't care if I'm making her feel like the scum of the earth. Love shouldn't hurt like this, and I didn't expect this kind of pain from my best friend. I thought I avoided these bullets. Trying to suppress my toxicity from pulling up on the ex, dropping him where he stands, and putting Gemini through a wall played over in my head every day. Knowing that she had this situation going on since Ferris days had me sick. This wasn't their first attempt at having a poly relationship together. I just thought it was over once I entered the picture. I want to air it all out but I'm going to stop for now before this ends up as a scene from "best man" (right hand on bible I'm not the one that's getting that ass beat.)

Weeks go by, and the sight of her face pisses me off but looking in my daughter's eyes gives me mixed emotions. I knew I had to move out because I could see the environment turning toxic. Most of our parents and grandparents will stay in this situation just for the kids, but you're damaging the kids even more in retrospect. They feel the energy of the two parents fighting and not being loving. Sometimes the best resolution is to part ways. I did everything I could do, I love a person so much I was willing to destroy myself. Most people never allow their love to flow that deep. Without fear, without remorse and without reciprocity I gave myself to someone. I tried and I enjoyed the ride, at least I got a daughter out the deal.

Shadow side (28)

"Never would I ever put you through this kind of pain. I think that is what hurts the most. But through the pain, I realize I need to move forward. but stuck with the thoughts of being in the middle of what I used to look forward to, keeps me suppressed leaves me duress in times of success I can't envision, don't want to make a decision, seeks permission from my heart to

My thoughts to switch the condition in which I continue to believe in these made-up fairy tales about love. It's the mission we all seek. But when it turns from love at first sight to bitch we don't speak, and it gets deep. Deeper than a family secret, more profound than a women's Intuition when she feels her man lying and deceiving. But yet we still seek it. It's our whole purpose to our existence. Growth and pain are, unfortunately, God's description of unlocking your higher self. I love me & I love myself, but this love shit???? Man, this something else. I charge it to the head, not my heart."

Months later, being in this space of separation but still living together was awkward. Free to do whatever we please left the window open for more hurt. Even with all the chaos going on, Gemini still had on the ring. I still hoped for us until the latest debacle. She and her ex had no contact supposably sense the last situation, but conversations were still being had. The information of us being separated enticed him to give it another try. so, they schedule a meetup to discuss what happened last time. (Just my Intuition) Not entitled to tell me anything, she decided to still lie about her whereabouts. For example, Both of our phones were located on the table, and one started ringing. I thought it was my phone, but it wasn't, it was her ex calling. Before that phone call, she told me she was going to hang out at the bar with some friends. But at that moment, I realized she was meeting up with him (Intuition)—no solid proof of my thoughts. I kept silent and allowed her to leave unchecked. When she got back home, I was already asleep. But when I woke up, I couldn't bottle my emotions anymore. I snapped at her for lying to me, and she confessed they kissed again.............. you probably guessed it right, dealing with a GEMINI is not for the weak and fragile.

<u>Chapter 11</u>
Clarity

At this point, this is something you want to pursue, so take my ring off; you don't deserve the love I have to give. That was my final breaking point. The first kiss was not the accident that she claimed it was. And I'm nobody's second option, I'm top tier, and I deserve that energy. All these thoughts are drowning me in depression, and not a single soul new. I was searching for answers.

I wish I could tell you this was the end of her bullshit, but it wasn't. After realizing we weren't a matching fit for each other I proposed a plan. I'll start looking for a new place to stay while she looks for a suitable job for her to maintain the apartment. We both agreed we would be respectful of each other's raw emotions In the chaos of a break up. I wouldn't bring any women to the house and she wouldn't bring any men. But of course, leave you to a Gemini to break that agreement. As soon as she felt secure with her job placement, she up a nigga with the quickness.

It was a Wednesday and I remember the moment vividly. The night before I had a vision of a guy's name. She was talking too in my sleep. I awakened like I was rising out of drowning water and it startled Gemini and she proceeded to ask me what was wrong. I asked her if she knew the name que? The look on her face was priceless, which gave me confirmation. My intuition was screaming to leave now, pack my stuff tonight because a storm is arising. I ignored it because I wasn't in position to leave. But In Reality, I wasn't ready for the reality of leaving the home I spent two and a half years creating for the family I thought I was going to have. She told me She knew of the name and the whole energy of what was left of the foundation vanished.

The following day it was around 9pm and my cousin called me and asked me to have some drinks with her at this restaurant up the street. I told her yea, I needed to get some fresh air. As I reach to put on my shoes, she's coming towards me with a surprised look on her face. She asked where I was going and I told her. She pleaded that she was about to leave and I needed to watch Athena. Of course, she had me fuck up and I firmly told her, well I'm already out the door you'll have to just cancel your plans until tomorrow, and I left. 13 min later I was at the restaurant chilling with my cousin and her friends' taking shots. With a roller coaster mind and a heavy heart my intuition was telling me to go back home. Everything just felt off and I was at the restaurant but it felt more like a sunken place. No longer being able to ignore my feelings I told my cousin I had to dip. The hour of fresh air did me well but it was something in the air and it was stuck (meaning it was an unresolved situation that needed to be addressed and until it's fixed it will be a problem).

Pulling up to my parking lot my ears started to ring uncontrollably. I noticed a white vehicle on the side of me and for a brief moment I thought I saw Gemini's face. My eyes said yes but my heart said "she wouldn't leave my daughter in the house by herself". I proceeded to go in the house, quiet. dark, both ears began to ring rapidly. I walked in the bedroom, no sign of Gemini. Walking in my daughter's room, she was sound asleep. My exact thought was that it was Gemini in that car when I pulled up.

Also, that's where she was headed before I left in the first place. She was outside with him the whole time I was gone. My brain cracked, my higher self-left my body and all I saw was red. I totally forgot I was on the phone with my spiritual friend the whole time. It was like we were talking in two different dimensions. Filled with my dark side I remembered my cousin left his gun at my house on top of the cabinet. I grabbed it, took the clip out to see how many bullets I had and snapped it back. Headed towards the door I had a forward vision of me walking outside and shooting that nigga car up. I shot the guy in the head and shot Gemini in the throat. She tried to get out of the car and I shot her point blank in the head. Then I went back into the house, covered in blood, grabbed Athena, took her to my moms and told her this was probably the last time she was going to see me.

Lucky that was just a vision but I felt it so deeply I heard my friend tell me to drop the gun and I did. Sat there for a min and made my way outside. I walked towards the car but as I was getting closer the car decided it wanted to drive off. My crazy ass stood in front of the car and demanded Gemini to get out of the car with the "come here" gesture. I looked at the man in the car with the look of "I'm not here for you, you're just here for pussy" and I nodded. Gemini gets out of the car and I light her ass up, I don't think I ever cussed someone out with that intensity. I took it there; I was officially that ghetto baby daddy with a ratchet baby momma. It made me sick to my stomach. Till this day she has no idea how close to death she was that night. Things should have gone left that night. I should be writing this book from jail cell instead of my bed. All thanks to God and I give thanks for giving me a second chance to choose my destined path. With nothing but my clothes and shoes I left everything. I let her keep everything I just wanted out. Her words to me that ended the conversation that night was "I've been ready for you to leave" like bitch I wasn't the gatekeeper for you to get your shit together. That was the very last time I would let anyone wound me like this. This is what happens when you love a soul that never learned how to love, pure survival mode.

"Fuel my (28) 🔥"

"The days seem shorter, weeks go by, and it doesn't even feel like you're getting older. Sleepless nights, consuming alcohol to feed your demonic spirits because feeding your inner devil numbs the pain. Fuels the flame, anything that will keep you from truly healing. Love isn't a sprint. It's a marathon. Everyone wants to run but didn't take the time to develop the proper leg strength to go the extra mile. who wants to run for hours to get the same prize you can win in seconds. Without the extra pain, without the extra strain, the marathon is long. You might even get to a point where you don't want to Win you just want to finish. Have you ever had a dream, but you gave it up to face reality? You spent years creating this image in your head of victory. Still, halfway through the dream, another runner passes you up, and another and another and another. until you get to space where defeat is Prevalent. Instead of kicking on that extra gear to fight to get back on top, you settle just to finish. I love love too much just to finish. I'm

sprinting the rest of the way, fuck flight I'm sprinting, even if I don't catch the other runners, I leave no doubt that I gave it my all. that's the dream, that's the victory that doesn't look pretty; losing and winning is one, and the same, perception is what helps fuel my flame. 🔥 "

My search led me to my true grand awakening; I spiritually hit rock bottom. With no place to go, I had to turn to myself. Everyone will reach a moment in their life when they have to choose the red pill or the blue pill. My blue pill was to continue the typical stereotype of a toxic baby father, bitter, angry, and ruin my child's mother's life every chance I got. Blame her for breaking up the family, being untruthful from the beginning without taking any fault of my own. Verbally abused her till I was blue in the face. I wanted her to feel lower than the soil. The red pill option was to sit back and listen. Understand this toxic relationship loop cycle I'm in and break free from it.

My ego wanted to take the blue pill, but my soul told me it was time to be a man and face my own created reality. The first step was to take accountability for me. I was so focused on living my dream that I never thought twice of what Gemini wanted. I was so hell-bent on a monogamous relationship with multiple kids and a housewife. Forget being on the same page. We weren't even in the same book. If going half on a baby was a person, that would be us. She wanted a baby so bad I never second guessed our mental head space with our prior engagements. If I knew she was still in love with another man, I wouldn't have chosen to get her pregnant. Our relationship was being forced, and the deeper we got involved romantically, the further we drifted away from our core foundation, which was our friendship. I was chasing unconditional love when I already had it. If she had told me her truths from the very beginning, I would have been more accepting of her loving someone else because I wasn't attached to the emotions of conditional love. Also, I had situations that I haven't given closure to.

      Things could have gone smoother, but then I would have missed the life lesson. I needed this situation to happen for me to be the most excellent version of myself. You can't control what another human being does, but you can control how you react and process it. Gemini used this beautiful analogy to describe my transition. "Most women leave their vase (Heart) on the table, and it gets knocked over constantly, and we just pick it back up and put it back on the table. Men put their vases on the top shelf so nobody can reach them, and once somebody does and knocks it over, the broken pieces remain on the floor. In my case, Gemini grabbed my vase on the top shelf and shattered it. Then she watched me slowly pick up the pieces, put the vase back together, and put it on the dining room table.

      2020 was a longgggggggg year. I lost a fiancé, and I almost lost my life in a car accident. I suffered depression and felt the lowest I ever felt in my life. But I choose not to stay in that low vibrational state. Love you. You can never lose love when you give yourself unconditional love. Love brought me out of my darkest moments if you let it, learn to quiet the ego noise that plays over and over again in your head and be still in the moment. Life is a constant change in perspectives. I didn't get heartbroken, my ego got exposed and crushed. My heart healed. The red pill opened my eyes and cracked the veil of my reality. I can't predict the future. Who knows if I find someone else? Should my best friend be my wife? Does Gemini find someone else? Do we get back together? Twin flame? All I know is whatever the situation is, I'm still healing, and nothing will ever take this black man's joy away again. My best friend is not my wife. She's my soul partner, maybe a twin flame, which will never change.

Raw (age 28)

"*Texting for hours in the same spot on the clock because you can't believe your reality. You were exchanging hurtful blows because the ego is wounded. You're not even listening to each other because everyone has to be right in their justification. What's love without some hate? The world must balance itself; you must balance yourself to align yourself with your true destiny...this human experience will continue to challenge you till you master the lesson; love is the most powerful human emotion and we as beings have yet master how to do it ... we're still figuring it out, that's why the divorce rate is 50%.... that's why being single is so much easier because the pain that comes with love is too much to bear...only fearful telling the truth of how you're going to make the other person feel but not the action itself .... we grew up in a monogamous world but just like Organized we are waking up into a different era, love is universal but 50% of us is stuck In the comfort of feeling like someone belongs to you when they don't, they belong to the universe and sooner you realize the easier relationships will be , you found happiness with another being and told yourself i want this person to make me and only me happy for the rest of my life and condition them to never love again, letting go of jealousy in this western view of marriage that's male dominated ... that's why you take his last name , Times is changing and if you don't unlearn what you thought was toxic and Society norms the better off you can be .. you can live in this world without feeling constant pain ... 50% of it is mentally inflicted, to be clinically Diagnosed as insane is doing the same action over and over again expecting a different result, expectations from humans is a set up for low vibrations .... raw truth isn't for the weak and the truth is we're here to experience love at its purist's form and it's limitless it's your choice to fall in love just beware that the love you crave is unconditional but you end up with conditions"*